THE COMPLETEPIANO TECHNIQUEBOOK

The Complete Guide to Keyboard & Piano Technique with over 140 Exercises

JENNIFERCASTELLANO

FUNDAMENTALCHANGES

The Complete Piano Technique Book

The Complete Guide to Keyboard & Piano Technique with over 140 Exercises

ISBN: 978-1-78933-209-4

Published by **www.fundamental-changes.com**

Copyright © 2020 Fundamental Changes Ltd.

The moral right of this author has been asserted.

All rights reserved. No part of this publication may be reproduced, stored in a retrieval system, or transmitted in any form or by any means, without the prior permission in writing from the publisher.

The publisher is not responsible for websites (or their content) that are not owned by the publisher.

www.fundamental-changes.com

Twitter: @guitar_joseph

Over 11,000 fans on Facebook: **FundamentalChangesInGuitar**

Instagram: **FundamentalChanges**

For over 350 Free Guitar Lessons with Videos Check Out

www.fundamental-changes.com

Cover Image Copyright: Adobe Stock / Africa Studio

Contents

Introduction	5
Get the Audio	6
Chapter One – Getting Ready to Play	**7**
Achieving Correct Height and Distance from the Piano	7
Moving Around the Keyboard	7
Hand Shape	10
Busy Fingers	11
Chapter Two – Fundamentals	**14**
Finger Action	14
Lifting the Fingers	14
Silent Finger Exercise	15
Strike and Release	16
It's All in the Wrist	16
Neutral Position	17
Down-Up Motion	17
Lateral Motion	19
Role of the Forearm	23
Rotation	25
Chapter Three – Legato and Staccato	**29**
Improving Legato Playing	29
Using the Wrist	31
Practicing Staccato and Building Technique	34
Staccato and Displaced Rhythm	35
Patterns Containing Skips	38
Chapter Four – Hand and Finger Independence	**41**
Different Note Durations	41
The Round	43
Different Articulations	44
Finger Independence	45
Chapter Five – How to Practice Scales and Arpeggios	**47**
The Movement of the Thumb	47
The Position of the Wrist and Forearm	47
Exercises for the Thumb	49
Learn the Fingerings First	50
A Good Place to Begin	50

Practicing Slowly with Raised Fingers	51
A Note About Arpeggios	52
Should Scales and Arpeggios Be Practiced Hands Together or Hands Separately?	52
Benefits of Playing Scales in Contrary Motion	53
Building Velocity	54
Arpeggios	57
Picking Up Speed	58
Summary of Practice Tips	59

Chapter Six – Double Notes — 60

Double Thirds	60
A Note About Playing Double Thirds Legato	62
Double Sixths	63
Sixths as a Prerequisite to Playing Octaves	67
Octaves	68
Application	69

Chapter Seven – Major Scales — 72

C Major Scale Fingering	72
Major Scales that do not use the C Major fingering	74

Chapter Eight – Minor Scales — 78

Minor Scales Organization	79
Scales that Use the C Major Fingering	79
F Minor and B Minor	81
Exceptions to the Rule	82

Chapter Nine – Major and Minor Arpeggios — 87

Group One	87
Group Two	92
Group Three	94
Group Four	97

Conclusion and Further Practice Tips — 98

Introduction

Welcome to the *Complete Piano Technique Book*. When learning piano, it is vital to perfect the techniques needed to play with ease, efficiency, and to avoid strain and injury. In order to enjoy a lifetime of playing, it's really important to have a solid technical foundation. With the correct foundation in place, we can focus wholeheartedly on playing the music we love – and the technical aspects will happen automatically.

The technique of playing piano involves so much more than simply hitting the right note at the right time! The act of playing involves the whole body, so in this book we will look in detail at how to achieve the right posture, position, and finger-wrist-arm playing technique.

You'll also learn the right way to execute the techniques you've heard professional pianists use to introduce light and shade into their playing and to create exciting or reflective moods.

Above all, this is a practical rather than a theoretical one, so it is packed with useful exercises, distilled over many years of teaching, that will help to refine your technique and make *you* the best pianist you can be. The exercises and practice suggestions in this book can be practiced as presented or can be applied to actual piano pieces on which you are working.

I hope you enjoy the journey and grow as a musician

Jennifer.

Get the Audio

The audio files for this book are available to download for free from **www.fundamental-changes.com.** The link is in the top right-hand corner. Click on the "Guitar" link then simply select this book title from the drop-down menu and follow the instructions to get the audio.

We recommend that you download the files directly to your computer, not to your tablet, and extract them there before adding them to your media library. You can then put them onto your tablet, iPod or burn them to CD. On the download page there are instructions and we also provide technical support via the contact form.

For over 350 free guitar lessons with videos check out:

www.fundamental-changes.com

Over 11,000 fans on Facebook: **FundamentalChangesInGuitar**

Tag us for a share on Instagram: **FundamentalChanges**

Chapter One – Getting Ready to Play

Believe it or not, height and distance have a tremendous effect on your piano playing. Sitting at the wrong height, too close, or too far away from the piano can not only cause discomfort but can even result in injury. Piano playing should never feel uncomfortable, so it is extremely important for us listen to what our bodies tell us.

Achieving Correct Height and Distance from the Piano

Often, people sit either too high or too low at their piano. The ideal height allows the hands, wrists, and forearms to be in a straight line as this position places the least amount of stress on the forearm where the muscles that move the fingers are located. Long tendons extend from these muscles through the wrist and attach to the small bones of the fingers.

If you sit too low, with your arms lower than the keyboard, you will constantly work hard to create a strong sound because you will be fighting their weight. If you sit too high, however, this will result in your fingers playing at an uncomfortable angle.

Sitting the correct distance from the piano allows you to access all the keys on the keyboard with ease.

Most people also tend to sit too close to the keyboard, which makes it more difficult to move from one piano register to the next because your arms are not able to freely move about. To check whether you're the correct distance away from the piano, see if your elbows can touch one another when your hands are placed on the white notes directly in front of you. If your elbows are unable to touch, move further back.

Moving Around the Keyboard

The first two exercises in this book will help you check your height and distance from the piano and should be played at whatever tempo is comfortable for you.

If you don't have an adjustable piano bench, try sitting on books or something solid to adjust your height. Play the exercises, make small adjustments to your height, and don't stop until you find what is most comfortable for you.

The exercise below is to be played using only fingers 1, 2 and 3 of your right hand. It might seem unusual, but the right hand often does cross over into the lower registers. As you play lower, lean your body to the left to help you gain better access to the notes.

Note that the *8va* sign written below the notes indicates that you should play the notes one octave below what is written.

Example 1a

How did you find playing the notes in the low registers? Were you able to reach all the notes?

If you found that you needed to slide yourself up or down the piano bench to reach the lower notes, try sitting closer to the front edge of the bench. This allows more space between the front of the bench and your legs, and allows you to lean toward the lower register and reach those lower notes more easily.

Next, we will do a similar exercise but now using the left hand. This exercise again uses fingers 1, 2 and 3 and is based on the notes C, D and E played in all registers above middle C. As you play higher lean your body to the right to help you gain better access to the notes.

The *8va* sign written above the notes in measures 3 and 4 indicates to play the notes one octave higher than written.

Example 1b

Once you are comfortable playing the previous two exercises, try the next exercise that uses alternating hands. The exercise is based on a broken C Major chord (notes C E G) which you will play from low to high and back down again.

Begin by leaning your body to the left. Once your hands arrive at the middle you should be sitting up straight. When your left hand moves past the middle of the keyboard, you will start leaning to the right.

Set the metronome so that an 1/8th note is equal to 200bpm.

Note: *LH* indicates the left hand, and *RH* indicates the right hand.

Example 1c

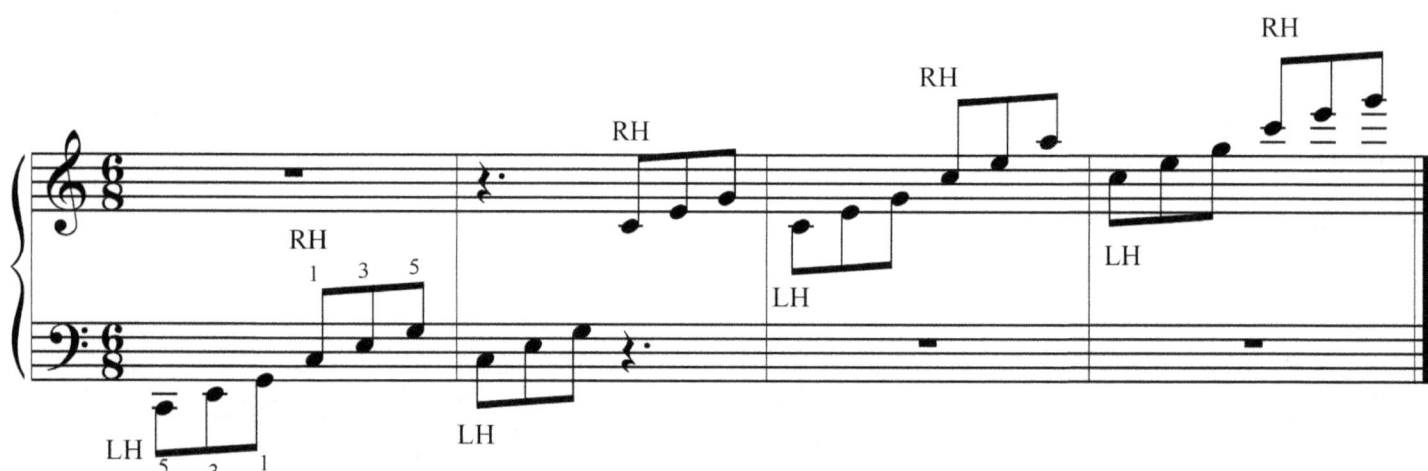

Now reverse the exercise to play the notes descending and begin by leaning to the right. Your body follows the direction of the notes.

Example 1d

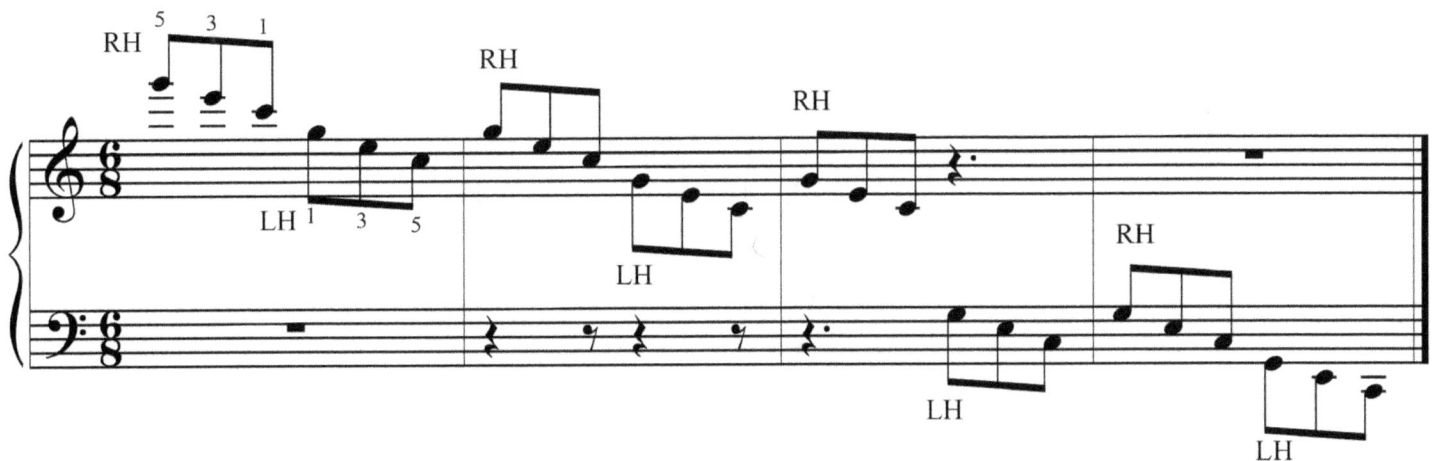

You can easily practice this exercise with different broken chords, such as a G Major (G B D) and an F Major (F A C). More experienced players can practice this exercise with all 12 major chords.

Pay attention to how your body moves as you play in the wider registers, compared to when you play in the middle of the keyboard.

Hand Shape

Developing the correct hand shape is the next step, so let's start with a simple exercise to make sure you're on the right track. To begin, hold out one of your hands in front of you, stretching out your fingers as far as you can.

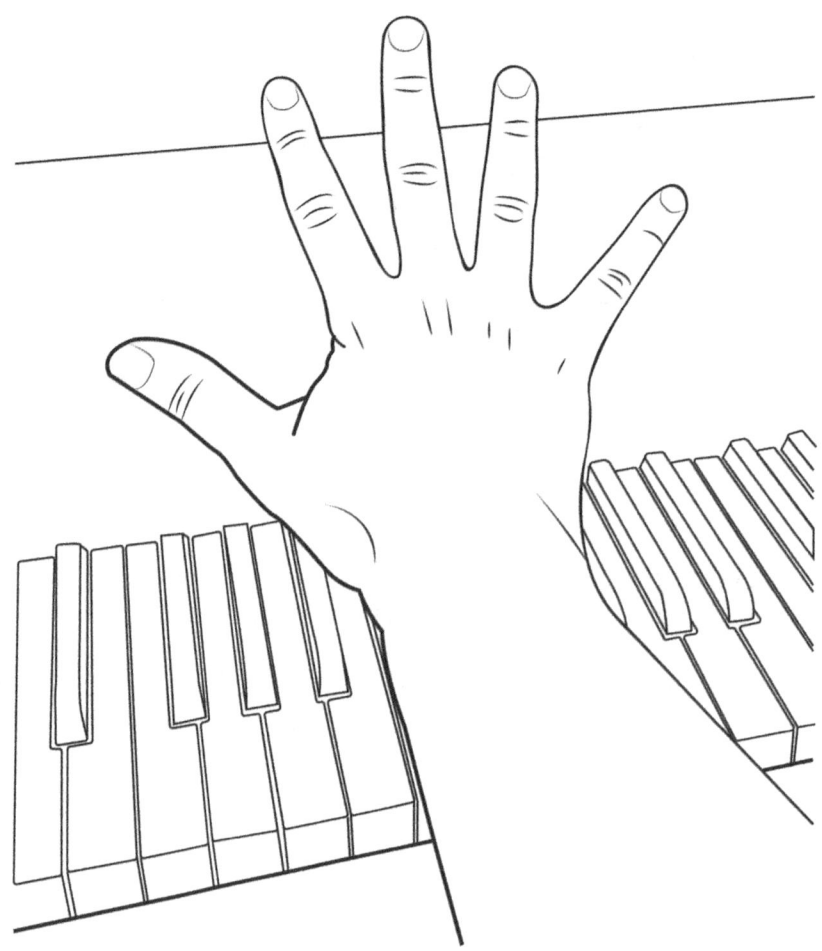

Hold your hand in that position for a few seconds and notice what happens. Do you start to feel the tension in your wrist and hand? You might notice that some tension began to move up your arm as well.

This is what you will experience if you play piano with an improper hand shape. The fingers work best when they are curved not straight. Hold out one of your hands and imagine someone handing you a tennis ball. This is the shape you want. However, don't grip the ball too tightly. Treat it as if it were made of thin glass to remind you that your hand must be relaxed while playing

Your hand should look like this:

And never like this:

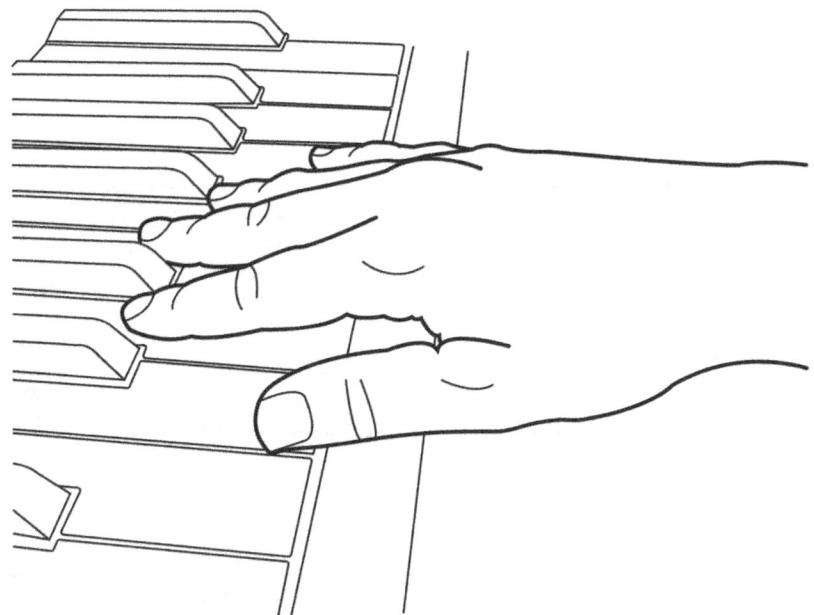

Busy Fingers

This example uses a simple five-note scale exercise to show you the importance of a good hand shape when playing the piano. First play it with straight, flat fingers, then play it using relaxed, curved fingers as described above. You'll find playing with curved, relaxed fingers is a lot easier.

Example 1e

Playing with curved fingers allows you to play faster, with more freedom, and much less tension. It feels more comfortable because it allows all the joints in the fingers to work together to create a quick finger action and smoother playing.

The next exercise shows how easily the fingers can play notes in quick succession when they are curved as opposed to straight. It can be played by each hand individually rather than both simultaneously if you're struggling.

Set the metronome to 80bpm and count the time out loud.

Example 1f

NOTE: Make sure that the smallest joints closest to the fingernails remain curved and do not cave in. This is very common and must be avoided. Look at the image below and notice the collapsed joint on the index finger. Avoid this!

By now you should realize how much your fingers can accomplish when they are curved properly.

Chapter Two – Fundamentals

How does one play the piano? What other parts of the body are involved? Many professionals will tell you that they feel the muscles working in many areas of their bodies – their shoulders, back, core and even their feet. This is often difficult for students to imagine, so to keep things simple I will focus on the three parts of the body that are *always* involved in playing piano: the fingers, the wrist and the forearm.

Finger Action

We have already discussed the importance of a good hand shape to allow for easier playing. Playing with curved fingers allows the fingers to move much more quickly. When we play piano, our fingers should look like little hammers or spider legs.

Finger exercises are practiced slowly to strengthen the small muscles in the hand and fingers, and this also allows us to be mindful of how the fingers work. Remember, the fingers, wrist and forearm all work together as a unit when we play. The stronger the fingers become, the better they work in harmony with the wrist and forearm.

Lifting the Fingers

All your fingers (including the thumb) should strike the piano keys with an identical movement so as to produce a consistent tone. Each finger is deliberately lifted and pressed down firmly. Then it is important to relax the fingers after striking the key to prevent tension building up inside the hand.

Let's break down the process into three short steps.

1. **Prepare – deliberately lift finger:**

2. **Strike** – press the key firmly:

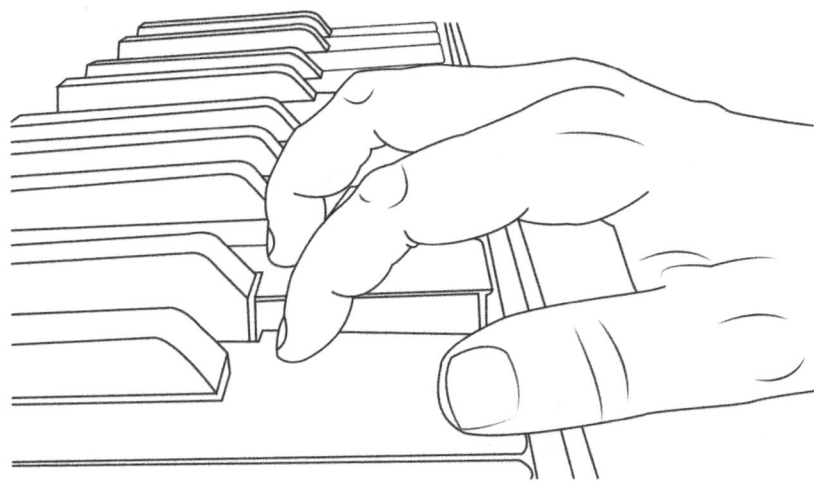

3. Release – immediately relax the muscles in hand and fingers while still keeping a good finger grip on the key that is depressed. Imagine you have a suction cup underneath your fingertip. Even though your hand should be relaxed, it should be difficult for me to push your finger off the keyboard.

Silent Finger Exercise

The goal of this exercise is to practice the basic finger movements. Place your right hand fingertips over the notes C D E F G and play this exercise without actually depressing the keys. Keep the fingers curved.

Example 2a

Now repeat this with your left hand beginning with your thumb on the note G.

Example 2b

Strike and Release

Exercise 2c is based on a five-note scale pattern and uses exaggerated finger movements to build strength. Use the same technique as before, but this time depress the keys fully and allow the notes to sound. Play very slowly, with the metronome clicking on the 1/8th note at 40bpm and play each line individually.

Note: The purpose of finger action exercises is to strengthen the hand and fingers so that they work correctly. The deliberate lifting of the fingers is not needed for most playing, but it is essential to practice this to develop good technique.

Example 2c

It's All in the Wrist

Imagine playing an expressive, lyrical melody. Some of the notes will be played louder while others might be softer. Wrist movement helps provide direction and contour to the melody by letting us control how much volume we produce.

When we allow the wrist to drop down, the weight of the forearm allows us to add more depth and substance to the sound of the notes. The weight of the forearm naturally makes our wrists drop down. When this happens, the notes become strong without being too harsh or percussive. When we raise the wrists, the notes become softer because we reduce the weight on the keys. This is one way to decrease the volume at the end of a phrase.

Neutral Position

In the previous chapter we learned that the default (neutral) position of the wrist is level with the forearm. The wrist, together with the hand and forearm form a straight, unbroken line.

Wrist in neutral position:

The wrist is never "locked" in this position and moves freely when we play the piano. These movements can be easily broken down into two types of motion: "down-up" and lateral.

Down-Up Motion

Down-up motion is when the wrist is lowered and raised.

Raised wrist:

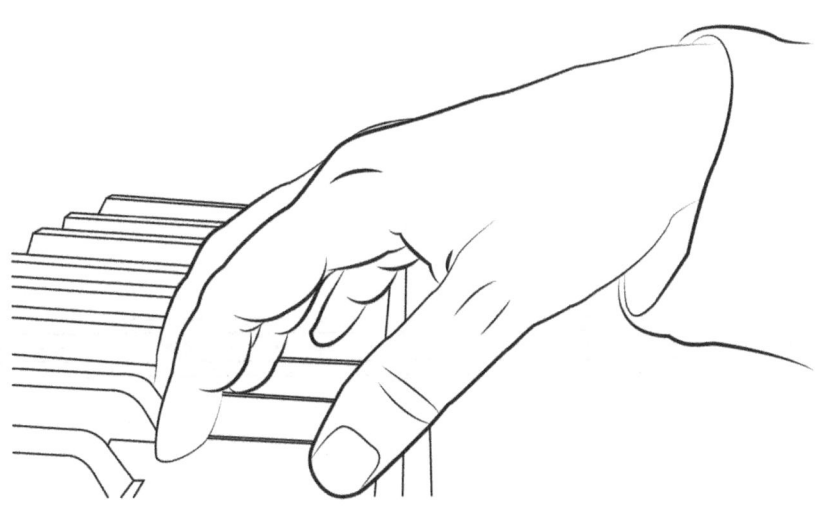

Lowered wrist:

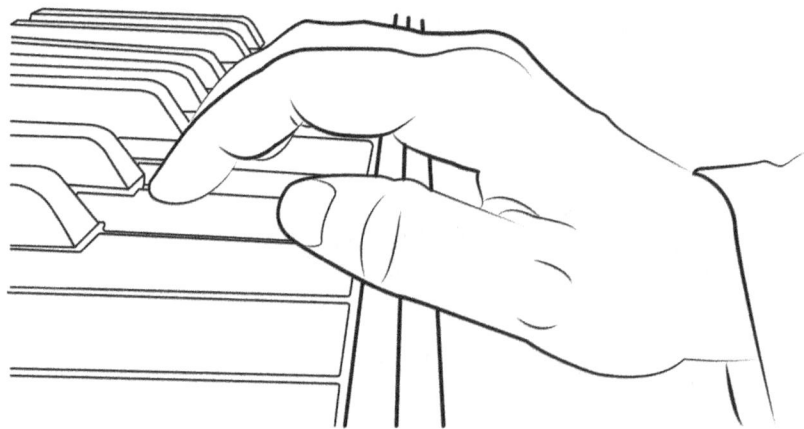

Look at Example 2d. Place your right hand on the keys with the wrist raised. On beat 1, play the first note with finger 1 while lowing the wrist. It should feel like you are "dropping" into the note. Let the note ring but on beat 2 raise the wrist. Lower it on beat 3 and raise it on beat 4. Repeat this with each finger on the remaining notes.

Reverse the exercise and repeat it with your left hand, beginning with the thumb on the note G.

The following three exercises should be played at 60bpm

Example 2d

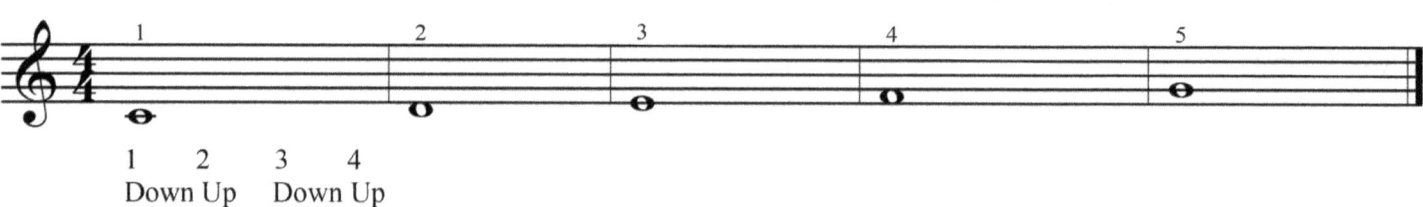

Example 2e

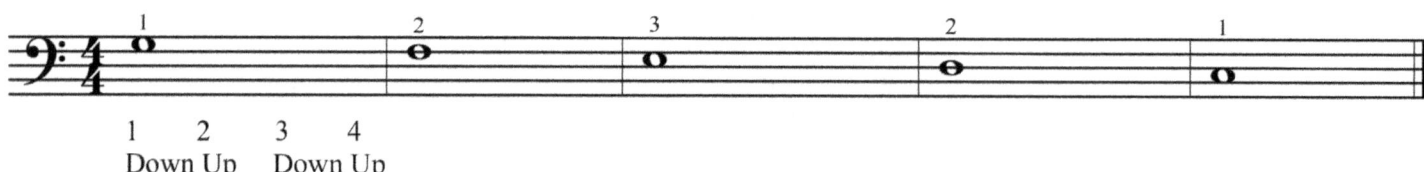

Now play exercise 2f, but lower and raise the wrist on the 1/2 notes. The wrists should be low on counts 1 and 3 and raised on counts 2 and 4. Play each hand in isolation before combining the parts.

Example 2f

Lateral Motion

Lateral motion occurs when the wrist moves from side to side and is necessary to bring the fingers into better alignment with the keys. When the wrist moves, the hand and forearm move along with it. Moving the wrist from side to side helps to distribute weight where it is needed.

This is what the wrist should look like when playing the first note of Example 2g with the right hand:

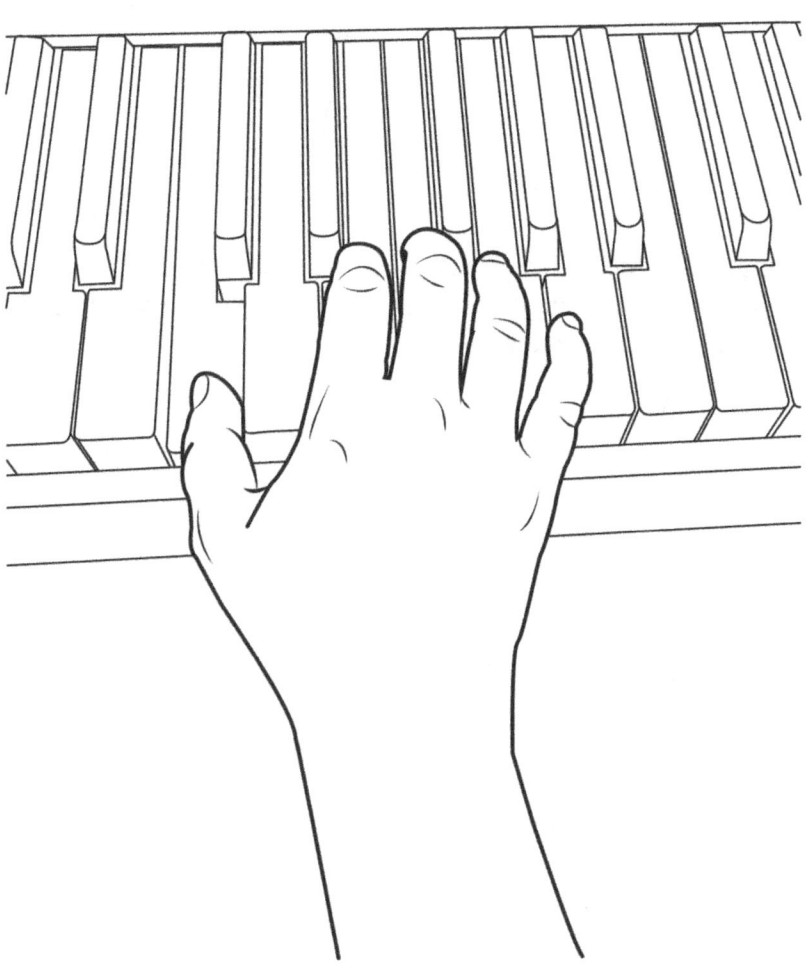

By the time the third note is played, the wrist should move to the right so that the weight can shift to the little finger:

Set the metronome to 60bpm. Play the exercise with your right hand first, then with your left, allowing each wrist to move freely from side to side. Once you become comfortable moving your wrists separately, you can practice the exercise with both hands simultaneously.

Example 2g

Note: Up-down and lateral motion often merge seamlessly into one movement. Example 2g spans a wider range of notes, and it is natural for the wrist to rise upward as it moves laterally towards the weaker fifth finger, allowing it to play with more strength. The merging of these two movements results in a kind of circular motion in the wrists.

It is important to ensure that you keep the fingers curved after they play each note, as straight fingers will create tension. The hand is like an elastic band and should only expand when it needs to. Notice how the hand should look once it reaches highest C note in the first measure:

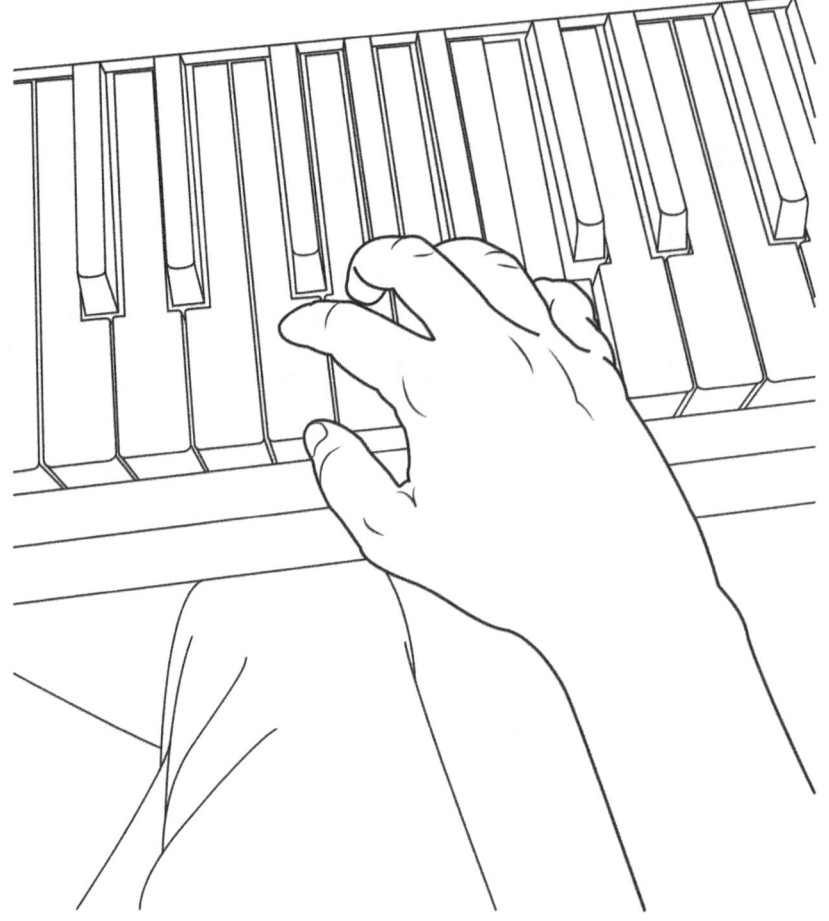

Keep these things in mind as you practice the exercise.

Example 2h

Now, let's play a similar exercise with the left hand.

Example 2i

Role of the Forearm

The forearm allows us to add weight to our playing and minimizes the percussive attack to achieve more sustain in the sound. This is because the added weight allows you to play deeper in the keyboard bed. Instead of thinking that you play a note by pressing or hitting a key, think of it more like kneading dough. Imagine a lump of dough that you need to flatten into a pizza. Think about how you would use your hands to flatten it. You will get more done with less effort by pressing down into the dough with your hands rather than by hitting it.

Your hands should not be stiff, but soft and relaxed, and the only time there should be any tension in the initial attack is when your muscles contract. With the help of your wrist and forearm, your fingers should press all the way down into the keys.

Play Exercise 2i beginning with a raised wrist.

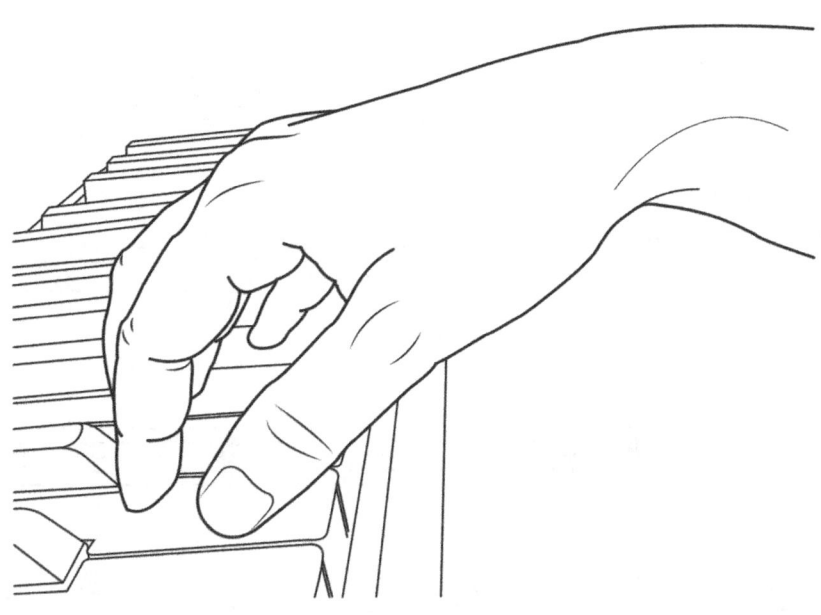

Then as you play the notes, push freely and deeply into the keys with the wrist falling as low as possible.

When you feel the weight of the arm, immediately release all tension. On the rest, the hand should be lifted from the wrist with the fingers hanging loosely from the keys.

Begin this exercise at 60bpm and make sure that all the notes sound simultaneously. Once you are comfortable, you can gradually increase the tempo and work up to 80bpm.

Example 2j

Note: Experiment with the speed at which you drop your wrists. The slower the wrist falls, the softer the sound. If you are a more experienced player, you can also try to create more volume by using muscles in your forearms. This will feel like you are pushing your wrists down as opposed to just letting them drop. Don't forget to release the tension once the wrists are down.

Rotation

The muscles of the forearms are involved in the movement of the fingers as well as the rotation of the hands. Rotation refers to the movement your hand makes when you turn it from palm facing down to palm facing up, like turning a doorknob. Like side-to-side wrist rotation, forearm rotation allows us to distribute weight in the hand to where it is needed.

We use rotation to play alternating notes. Below are two images of what the forearm rotation should look like when playing Example 2j.

The example begins with the pinky finger playing F.

Now compare that to when the second note is played.

See how the hand turns? Set the metronome to 80bpm and play Example 2k with your left hand using rotation. The movement should feel similar to that of turning a key or doorknob.

Example 2k

Play the exercise below being mindful of forearm rotation.

Set the metronome to 80bpm and gradually increase the speed over time up to 100bpm.

In examples 2l, 2m and 2n, learn the right hand first, then the left. Once you feel comfortable playing each hand separately, you can play both simultaneously.

Example 2l

Examples 2m and 2n are great for practicing forearm rotation

Example 2m

In the second half of the exercise the pattern is played descending the keyboard. When comfortable, you can practice example 2m and 2n hands together, although you should keep to a slow tempo.

Example 2n

28

Chapter Three – Legato and Staccato

There are many different ways notes can "speak" when we play the piano, and this is what we call *articulation*. You are probably already familiar with two types of articulation that we use in practice and performance: *legato* and *staccato*.

Legato is an Italian word that means *tied together* and indicates that the notes should be played connected and smoothly, so each note flows seamlessly into the next without any silence in between. Notes that are played legato are marked with a slur.

Example 3a

Staccato is an Italian word that means *detached*. Staccato is the opposite of legato in that there is silence between the notes. This effect is created by shortening the duration of each note so that a 1/4 note might sound more like an 1/8th note followed by an 1/8th rest.

Staccato is indicated by dots directly above or below the note heads.

Example 3b

Improving Legato Playing

When we play legato, we do not release the first note until after we have played the note that follows. A great way to practice legato is to play a phrase at a slow tempo and exaggerate this overlap. This process helps your fingers to learn not to release notes too soon.

Example 3c is a five-note scale played in the right hand. Set your metronome to 40bpm and play perfectly in time, connecting each note to the next. Play the first note as normal, but then play the second note while still holding down the first.

While you have the two keys pressed down, take a moment to listen to the two notes sounding together and then release the first note, allowing the second to sustain by itself.

Example 3c

Now follow the same steps for Exercise 3d in the left hand.

Example 3d

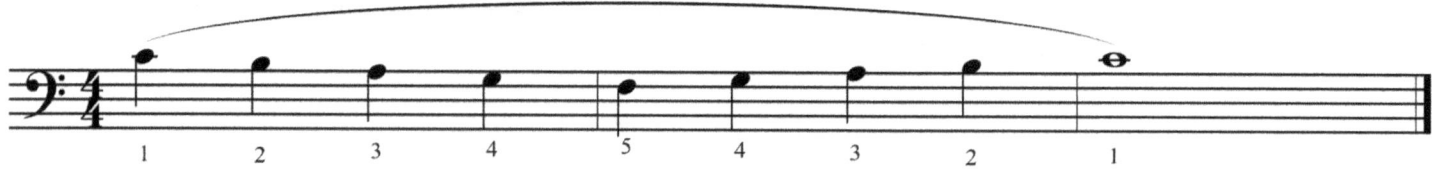

Play exercises 3e and 3f in the same way. Once you feel more confident in your playing, you can gradually increase the tempo to 100bpm. Pay close attention as you play to ensure that each note flows into the next.

Example 3e

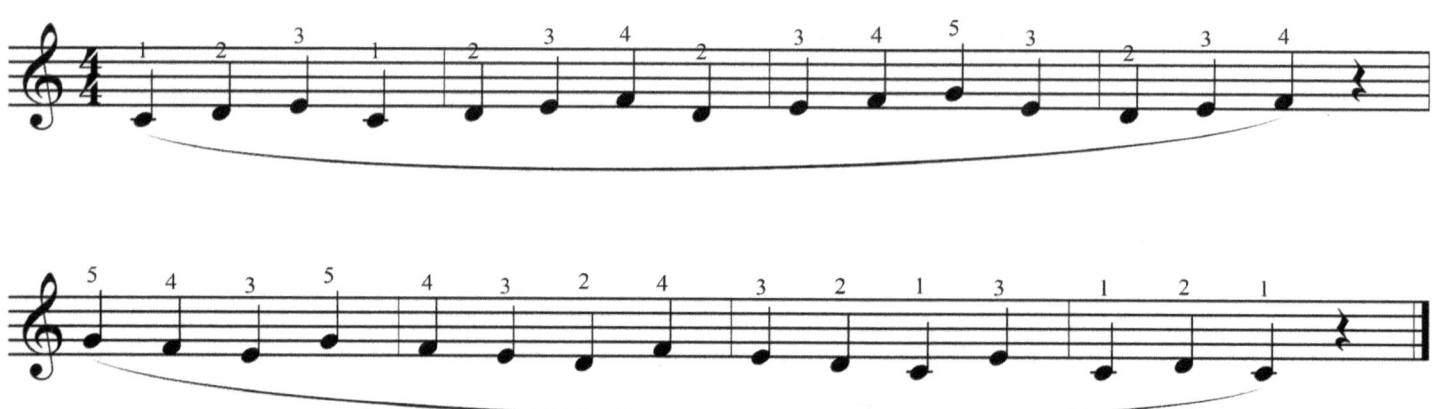

Example 3f

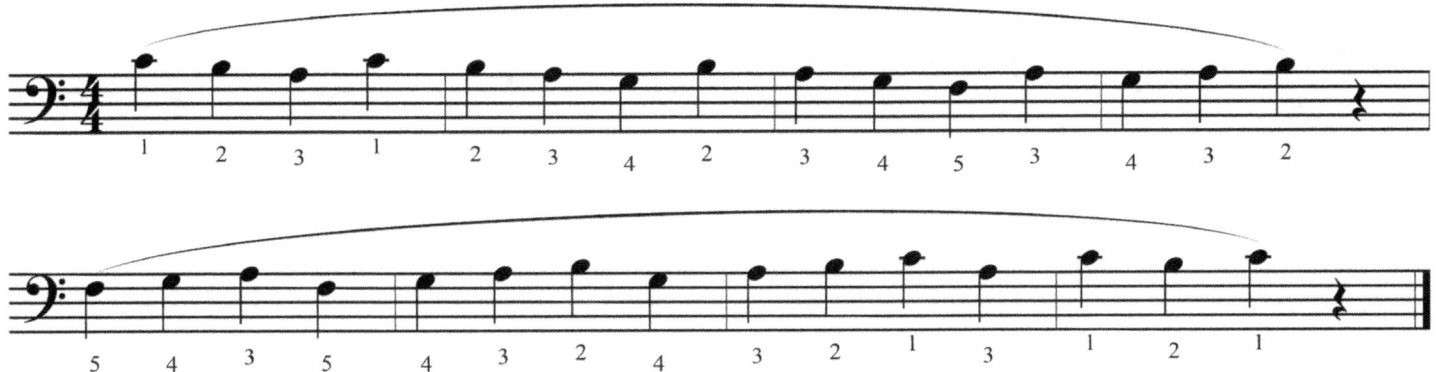

Using the Wrist

Slurs join two or more notes together. We play the notes within the slur legato, but we also play the notes within a slur with one wrist movement. Exercises 3g and 3h contain two notes within each slur.

In the previous chapter we studied the down-up wrist movement, and this technique is regularly used when playing legato to give the melody a more musical shape.

To play the two-note slurs:

1. Begin with your wrist raised

2. Drop into the first note

3. Lift the wrist as you play second note.

The first note should sound stronger than the second note. As you play these exercises think "down-up" or "loud-soft."

Before playing the following right hand exercise, study the first measure and get a sense of dropping the relaxed wrist into the first note and lifting it off on the second. The first note should sound strong while the second note should be lighter. Set your metronome to 80bpm and as you play the two-note slur, think "heavy-light."

Once you are comfortable playing the first two-note slur, play each pair of slurred nots with a pause in between. There's no need to play strictly in time, just try to develop a feel for how the wrist should move and how the notes should sound. Listen to the audio track to help you.

Finally, play the complete exercise in time without the pauses. Ensure that after your wrist lifts while playing the second note of the pair it is ready to drop into the first note of the next one.

Example 3g

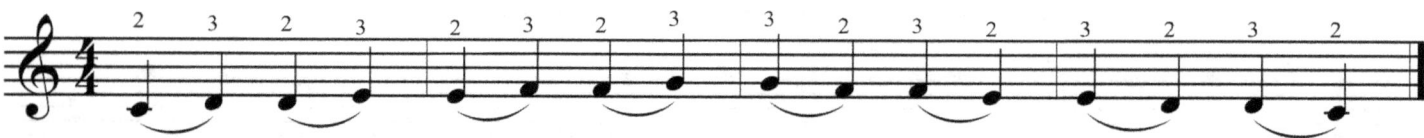

Now repeat the exercise below using the left hand.

Example 3h

Practice the two previous exercises with different fingerings. Try using fingers 1 and 2, 3 and 4, and 4 and 5.

Note: Listen to the first movement of Beethoven's *Sonata in D minor, Op. 31, No 2 "Tempest"*. It uses a lot of two-note slurs.

The following exercise contains both two-note and three-note slurs and should be played at 80bpm.

Three-note slurs begin the same way as two-note slurs – by dropping into the first note. However, the wrist will rise more slowly because you are playing two notes on the way up. However, the wrist will still finish in a high position after playing the third note. As you play this exercise think "down-rise-up." The first note will be the strongest, and the third will be the softest.

Before playing through the exercise, isolate the three-note slurs first to get a feel for how to play them. Note that the three notes within each slur are played legato, but you should hear a tiny space or "breath" between each group.

Example 3i

The final exercise contains a four-note slur and the same wrist movement applies. After you drop into the first note, you must play three notes as the wrist rises back up. Your wrist might even begin to rise after playing the third note instead of the second – it just depends on how fast or slow you play the example.

Although this exercise contains 1/16th notes, that doesn't mean it should be practiced fast. Use the same 80bpm tempo as the previous exercises and gradually increase the speed as you improve.

Example 3j

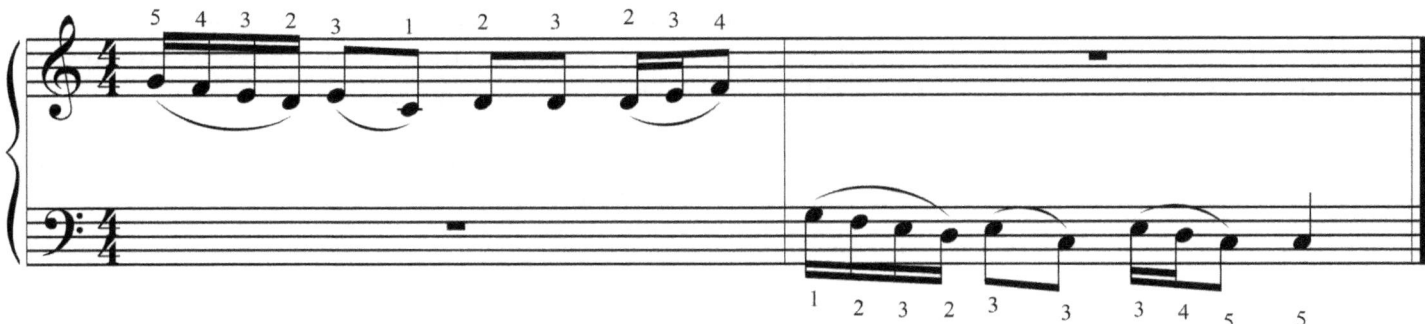

Note: Slurs can contain any number of notes and these are all approached the same way. Always allow the wrist to drop into the first note of the slur and lift on the last note.

A phrase is like a sentence. When we speak, we do not say each word the same way. The volume of our voice changes, which allows us to sound expressive. The same is true for music and how the notes "speak" on the piano. Often there is a decrease in volume at the end of a musical phrase.

Perfecting our wrist movement is essential because it helps us control the sound and vocal quality of the phrase. By dropping into the notes, we can make them sound strong, and by playing the notes as we lift the wrist, we can lower the volume at the end of a phrase.

As you become more comfortable with examples 3g through 3j, gradually increase the tempo and work towards 100bpm. If you are a more experienced player, make the exercises more challenging by transposing them into different five-note finger positions. Try playing them in the keys of G, D, A and E.

Application: Go through some piano pieces you are currently studying or use some of your all-time favourites. Apply the techniques in the previous exercises to any legato sections you come across, or simply play what's written as legato.

Imagine you are singing the melody. How would it be sung? Where would the singer breathe? Even if the piece consists of a long, luscious melodic line, you can still apply these techniques. Practice the melody with an exaggerated legato as we did at the beginning of this chapter.

If your pieces contain slurred notes in smaller groups, work with one group at a time and allow the wrist to work with you. Besides keeping the hand relaxed, it will help you to create a singing melody that builds and fades with each phrase.

Practicing Staccato and Building Technique

Practicing any finger exercise staccato helps strengthen the muscles in the fingers and firm up our fingertips. Being able to produce a clean, crisp staccato is much more difficult than getting a velvety legato because it requires more finger control.

Often when passages call for staccato playing, the pianist may use a lighter touch, but as with the legato exercises, we will be exaggerating to develop a strong, powerful, yet controlled staccato.

In the following exercises, the finger will quickly strike the key with force, then pull inward towards the palm of the hand. Think of it as a quick flicking movement, like a cat scratch, that will allow each note to sound short and crisp. After each strike, you must immediately release any tension in the hand or fingers. These exercises should be played slowly, allowing enough time between the notes for the muscles to relax.

Play the following exercises with your metronome set to 60bpm. Exercises written in treble clef are to be played with the right hand, and those written in bass clef are to be played with the left.

Example 3k

Example 3l

Now set your metronome to 100bpm and play the exercises faster. You can practice this with passages even if they are *not* marked staccato – it's a great way to practice scales or any passage in a piece of music that needs to be cleaned up. It also helps to firm up your fingers!

Practicing staccato not only builds finger technique but it also reinforces fingerings. If you find yourself making many mistakes in scale-like passages, often this is because you are not secure in your fingering. When you practice these passages staccato you can focus on ensuring you are consistent in the fingerings you use. This will strengthen your musical memory and make your playing more automatic.

Staccato and Displaced Rhythm

We all want to play flourishes of notes at lightning speed, but how do we play quickly while performing with a clean, even touch? One answer is to practice using a *displaced* rhythm. To begin, let's examine this exercise which is based on this five-finger pattern.

Example 3m

One way to build muscle memory so that our fingers can play this exercise accurately at quicker tempos is to use staccato with the two different rhythmic patterns shown in examples 3n and 3o. Listen to the audio to hear how they should sound.

Example 3n

Example 3o

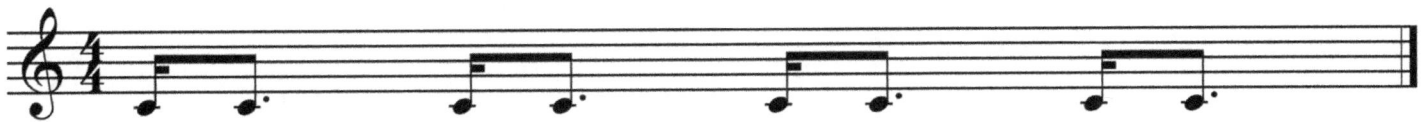

Although the following exercises show both hands playing simultaneously, I highly recommend first practicing each hand individually, especially if these concepts are brand new to you.

The goal here is to play the notes in quick succession two at a time. Think of long notes and short notes. The shorter notes will "snap" into the longer ones.

Example 3p

In Example 3q, we take these same exercises and flip the rhythms around to begin with the 1/16th note instead of the dotted 1/8th. This changes the two-note combinations so that the first note, C, will snap into the second note, D.

Ensure you relax after each dotted 1/8th note and practice this exercise slowly at 40bpm.

Exercise 3q

Next the exercises are written in regular 1/8th notes. Set the metronome to 100bpm and play them as written. You can play the left hand and right hand alone instead of simultaneously if you wish.

Example 3r

Using displaced rhythms is a great way to practice scales in any passage that has a long string of notes. They will teach you to play all the notes evenly and help you develop a cleaner touch.

Apply the concepts from the second half of this chapter to the exercise below. Again, don't play the left and right hand parts simultaneously; first learn the right hand and then work with the left in these three steps:

1. Set the metronome so that the 1/8th note is equal to 60bpm. Practice the exercises as you did in example 3k through 3l with a sharp staccato touch to firm up the fingertips.

2. Set the metronome so that the 1/4 note is equal to 40bpm. Use the same type of staccato touch but with displaced rhythm as we did in examples 3p and 3q.

3. Set the metronome so that the 1/4 note is equal to 100bpm and play the exercises as you normally would.

Example 3s

Patterns Containing Skips

The exercises presented in the second half of this chapter all contain notes that move in stepwise motion. The following exercises are different in that they also contain skipping notes. Practicing exercises such as these will help isolate and strengthen all of the fingers.

The pattern for the following two exercises (Examples 3t and 3u) is based on the tenth exercise found in Hanon's *Virtuoso Pianist in 60 Exercises.* This pattern begins with a large skip followed by notes moving down in a stepwise manner. Examples 3t presents the pattern ascending and Example 3u descending.

Examples 3v and 3w are based on a pattern of melodic thirds.

For these exercises, work the hands separately and make sure to follow the suggested fingering introduced in the first measure. Follow the same procedure suggested for Example 3s.

Example 3t

Example 3u

Example 3v

Example 3w

Chapter Four – Hand and Finger Independence

Sometimes playing piano can feel like you're scratching your head and rubbing your tummy, because both hands normally play different things at the same time. Sometimes two different things can happen in the same hand, such as playing a melody while holding down notes to provide harmonic support. In this chapter we will look at some exercises to help you develop this independence between your hands and fingers.

Different Note Durations

Often you will find yourself playing faster notes in your right hand while playing slower notes in the left.

Examples 4a through 4d are based on a five-note C Major scale pattern. The first two examples contain one hand playing 1/8th notes while the other plays 1/2 notes. The next two examples contain one hand playing 1/8th notes while the other plays 1/4 notes.

When your hands are doing different things, often one hand wants to shadow what the dominant hand is doing.

Learn these exercises in the following way:

1. Learn each hand separately first to become comfortable with fingering.

2. Set your metronome to 80bpm. Play the right hand while tapping with rhythm of the left hand with the left, and vice versa.

3. Set the metronome to 60bpm and play hands together. As you become more confident, gradually increase the tempo in 8bpm increments.

Example 4a

Example 4b

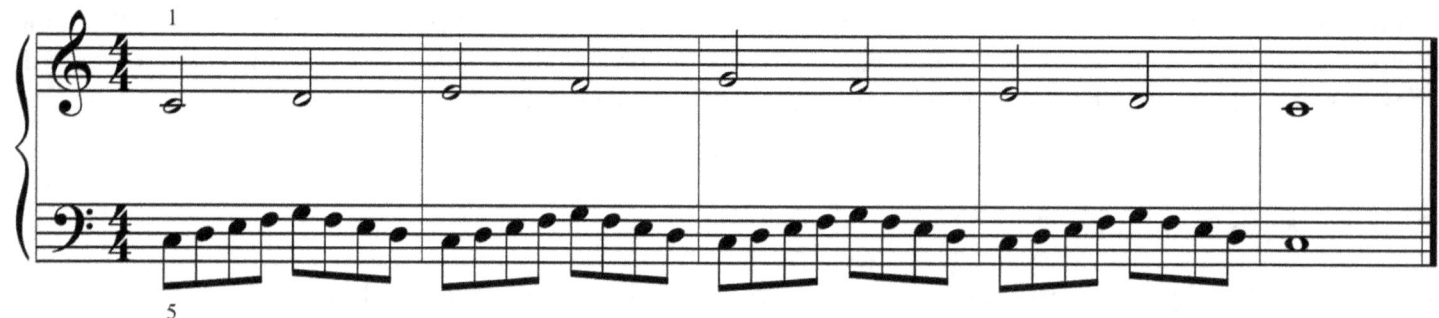

Example 4c

Example 4d

If you are a more experienced player, add dynamics to the previous four exercises. Play the right hand *forte* (loud) while the left plays *piano* (soft), and vice versa. While in many cases the right hand plays louder than the left (because it's playing the melody), it is not uncommon that the left hand plays the melody while the right hand provides harmonic support.

The Round

There are often times when one hand will play a melody and the other hand will repeat it a measure or so later to create a kind of musical dialogue. In music, a "round" is a song that can be sung by two or more groups of people. One group starts, then the next group joins in by singing the same part a bar or two later.

The next two examples are based on the children's tune *Frère Jacques*. Example 4e begins with the right hand, which is followed by the left hand two measures later. In Example 4f, the left hand leads and the right hand follows.

Follow the same practice method as you did in examples 4a through to 4d.

Example 4e

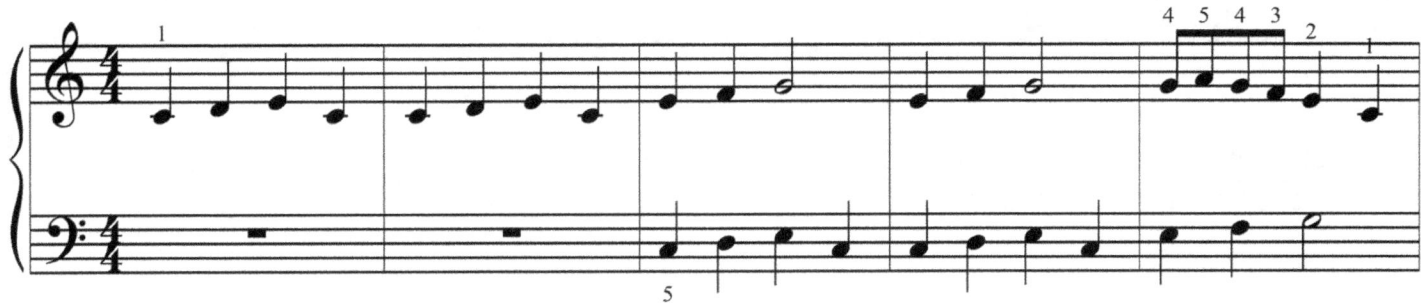

Example 4f

Learning this type of technique will prepare you for playing the music of J.S. Bach, starting with his *Inventions*, which is a collection of short piano pieces that consist of two independent melodies or voices (one played by each hand) that work together to complement one another. Bach's *Sinfonias* take things up a notch because they consist of three voices. Finally, the most sophisticated and challenging of Bach's work are his *Well-Tempered Klavier,* which consist of 24 Preludes and Fugues

Different Articulations

Sometimes our hands don't play the same kind of articulation. For example, the right hand may play a legato melody over a left hand staccato accompaniment. The next two examples help you prepare for this type of musical situation.

Begin these exercises at 60bpm to allow time for the hand that plays staccato to release each note. It helps to imagine that the staccato notes are not 1/4 notes, but 1/8th notes separated by an 1/8th rest. Keep in mind that you can use a lighter staccato touch here. The exercise should not sound like the exercises in the previous chapter.

As you become more comfortable playing these two examples, gradually increase the tempo by increments of 8bpm. See if you can gradually reach 100bpm.

Example 4g

Example 4h

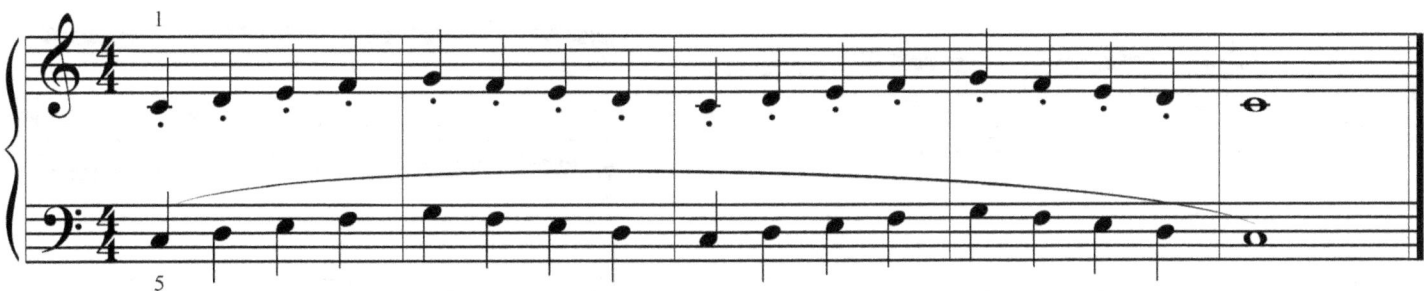

Note: The second movement, of Beethoven's *Sonata in D Major, Op. 28 "Pastorale"*, has a legato melody in the right hand played against a staccato accompaniment in the left.

Finger Independence

Our hands are not limited to playing just a single line melody at one time, and we often have to play the melody and harmony in the same hand. Sometimes we may even have to play more than one melody line in one hand.

Example 4i consists of a series of "holding" exercises that help to train your fingers for these situations and will help you develop finger control and independence in each hand. Set your metronome to click on the 1/8th at 40bpm and practice these exercises slowly.

Play the first whole note by dropping into it like you have nothing else to play after it. Then keep that note held down while you play the other notes in the measure. If this is new to you, move away from the keyboard and practice it on a table top to help you to train the fingers independently. Once you become used to how the fingers move, return to the exercises to the piano.

Again, the exercises have been combined to save space. Practice each measure separately. Also, practice the left and right hands separately. It is not necessary to play this exercise hands together.

Example 4i

Chapter Five – How to Practice Scales and Arpeggios

When we learn to write, letters come together to form words, and those words start to form sentences. Imagine learning how to write without knowing the names of the letters of the alphabet! If we didn't have any understanding of the letters, how could we create words or sentences? The same is true with music. Knowing your scales and arpeggios is like learning the letters and first words of music.

A scale is the tonal basis of music. It is a series of notes from which melodies and harmonies are built. Arpeggios are simply chords that are played one note at a time. Learning your major and minor scales, and your arpeggios will not only build your technique as a pianist, it will help you understand how music is organized.

Learning the major and minor scales and arpeggios is essential for anyone who is serious about studying classical piano. Jazz pianists take things a step further and learn other types of scales such as the diminished, major pentatonic, minor pentatonic, blues, and modal scales. Regardless of what type of music you play, knowing your scales and arpeggios inside out will be a great benefit to you.

The Movement of the Thumb

The thumb is a unique finger because besides being able to move up and down, it can easily move from side to side. One of the biggest challenges we face when we begin to learn scales and arpeggios is building mobility in the thumb.

What do I mean by mobility? Let's use the C Major Scale as an example. Below we have an ascending C Major Scale played by the right hand.

The thumb plays the first and fourth notes and must begin its journey under the 3rd finger the moment the 2nd finger plays the D note. If the thumb begins to move any later than this, it will be forced to rush under the fingers and will cause the elbow to jerk up and down. The elbow should never do this because your scale and arpeggio playing should be smooth. The hand should always glide smoothly and never jerk quickly into an awkward position.

Example 5a

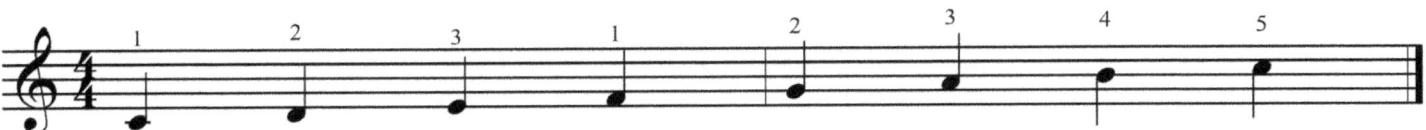

The Position of the Wrist and Forearm

When we practice scales and arpeggios, we often focus only on what our fingers are doing and don't consider the position of the wrists and forearms in relation to the keyboard. We often play scales with our fingers, wrist and forearms running parallel to the keys as shown below.

This is fine when you are playing towards the center of the keyboard – for example, when the right hand is descending and the left hand ascending, and the fingers cross over the thumb. The thumb naturally moves sideways here and easily allows the hand to move into a new playing position.

However, when you are playing away from the center of the keyboard, it is best to angle the hand, wrist and arm away from the body at about a 45-degree angle. This allows the thumb to easily pass under the fingers without the hand jerking sideways to access a new playing position, as shown below.

Allow the elbow and forearm to lead and move slightly ahead of the hand. Wherever the forearm goes, the wrist and fingers will follow. The fingers, wrist and forearm should all glide smoothly across the keyboard and the elbow should never jerk up and down.

Exercises for the Thumb

If scales and arpeggios are relatively new to you, here are some exercises to help increase the movement and flexibility of the thumb, allowing it to easily pass under the fingers.

Play each of these exercises with each hand separately and the metronome set at 60bpm. Remember the following:

1) When the hands play away from the center (RH ascending and LH descending), keep your hand at about a 45-degree angle in relationship to the keyboard.

2) When the hands move away from the center (RH descending and LH ascending), position your hands and wrists so that they run parallel to the keys on the piano.

When first practicing these exercises, play one note per beat and once you become comfortable, increase the speed gradually towards 80bpm.

Example 5b

Example 5c

Example 5d

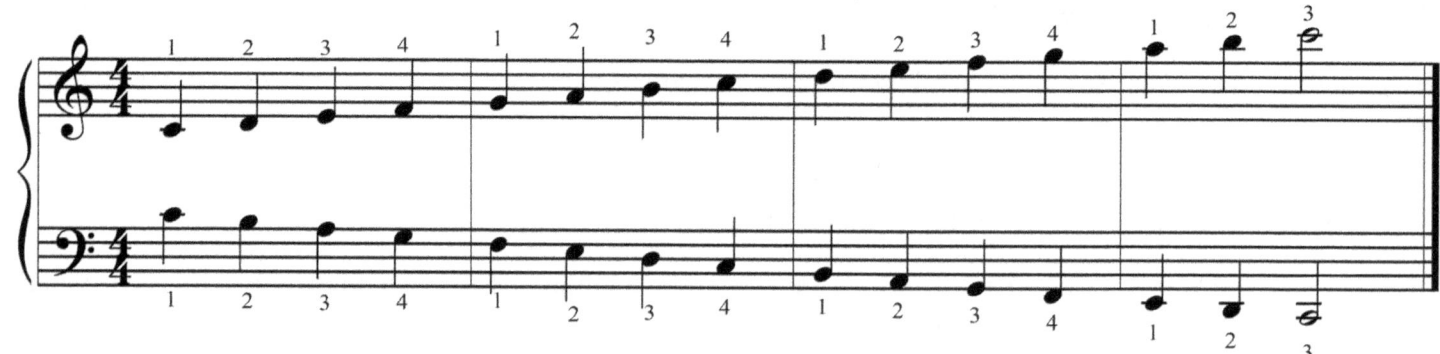

Learn the Fingerings First

Before you begin working on scales and arpeggios, it is important to learn which fingers play each of the notes. Chapters seven to nine contain fingerings for the major and minor scales and arpeggios as a reference if you need them.

A Good Place to Begin

Most students usually learn the C Major Scale first because it doesn't contain any sharps or flats, and is made up of only white keys. However, this actually makes it physically more difficult to play, as all the white keys are the same length and don't fit under the hand and fingers naturally.

A better choice for your first scale is B Major, because not only does it fit nicely under the fingers, the black keys make it easy to remember the fingering.

Begin by playing only the black notes in the scale. It's natural that when your hand is on a pair of two black notes, that you use fingers 2 and 3, and when your hand is over three black keys, you use fingers 2, 3 and 4. Play the example below a few times with your right hand first, then your left.

Example 5e

It is now easy to remember on which notes your thumb will land.

Now let's fill in the missing notes of the sale. In our left hand, notice that we start the scale on the 4th finger and this is logical based on the pattern of black keys.

Learn Example 5f at 60bpm and practice one hand at a time. Remember to angle your right hand away from your body as you ascend the scale, and your left hand away from your body when you descend.

Example 5f

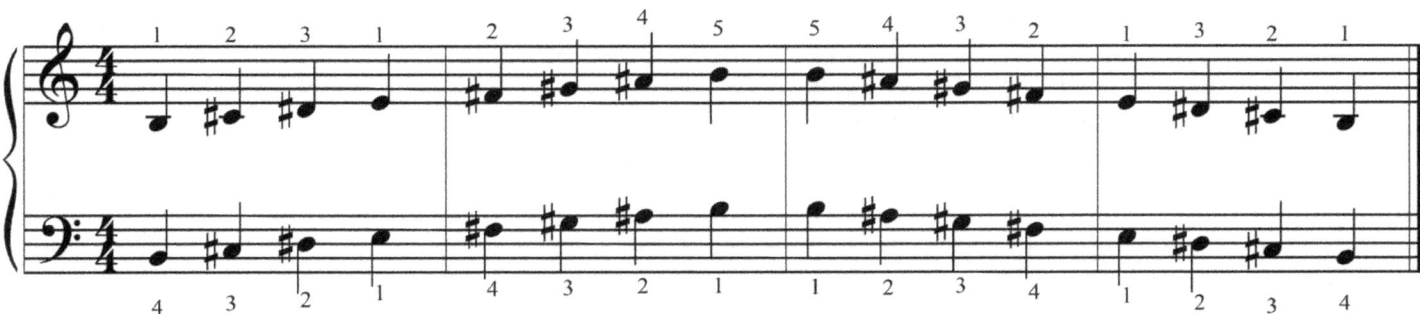

Practicing Slowly with Raised Fingers

You have now learned the fingering for one octave of the B Major scale. However, as a musician it is a good idea to be able to play several octaves of any scale or arpeggio. If you are relatively new to scales, playing two octaves is ideal and if you are more experienced, four octaves will do just fine.

Example 5g shows the B Major scale written in two octaves. Get familiar with the fingerings because once you can play a scale over two octaves, it's easy to span it across the entire keyboard if you wish.

Example 5g

Play each hand separately at a speed of 60bpm. The goal is to internalize the fingering in each hand while learning to play the scale slowly with ease.

Keep the following in mind:

1. When the hands play away from the center (RH ascending and LH descending) remember to keep your hand at about a 45-degree angle in relationship to the keyboard.

2. When the hands return to the center (RH descending and LH ascending) position your hands and wrists so that they run parallel to the keys on the piano.

3. As you play, deliberately lift the fingers before striking the keys. If you need a refresher on how to practice in this manner, revisit Chapter Two.

Note: The scale and arpeggio examples are written so that the hands play two octaves apart for easier reading. If you wish to practice *hands together*, you can play the left hand one octave higher.

A Note About Arpeggios

The challenge of arpeggios has to do with the thumb travelling a greater distance under the fingers. As in scale playing, it is best to angle the hand, wrist and arm away from the body, at about a 45-degree angle for ascending arpeggios in the right hand and descending in the left. This makes it easier for the thumb to pass under the fingers.

Should Scales and Arpeggios Be Practiced Hands Together or Hands Separately?

While many pianists practice scales and arpeggios hands together, there is a place for practicing them hands separately too. Practicing them hands separately allows you to quickly discover which hand needs more work and practice time. Often this is the left hand, since the right tends to be more active when playing. If you are a relative beginner and just learning the correct fingerings and motions for the scales and arpeggios, practicing hands separately will be very beneficial for you.

However, there are many benefits to practicing scales and arpeggios hands together. For example, you'll quickly develop independence between the hands because the fingering for each hand is different.

Below is a G Major scale. Read the fingering instructions carefully and you'll see that they are very different in the left and right hands.

Though both hands play the same notes you can see that each line begins on a different finger. In the right hand the thumb goes under and plays the note C, but the left hand plays it with the second finger. Because your fingers are doing two different things at the same time, this is a great way to build independence between your hands.

Example 5h

So, should you practice scales and arpeggios hands together or hands separately? I would suggest using a combination of both.

Benefits of Playing Scales in Contrary Motion

A good way to transition into playing scales hands together is to begin by practicing them in *contrary motion*. This is where the hands play in opposite directions. While the notes are different, in many cases the fingerings are the same.

Here is a G Major scale played two octaves in contrary motion.

Example 5i

Contrary motion sounds more pleasing to the ear than parallel motion and it occurs often in music. You will find that the melody in the right hand often moves in contrary motion to the bass in the left. Even though both hands are playing the same fingering, contrary motion allows for more independence between the parts and makes the music more interesting.

The scales that have symmetrical fingerings when played in contrary motion are C Major, D Major, E Major, G Major, A Major and their parallel minors.

Building Velocity

In Chapter Three we discussed the benefits of practicing staccato and saw how it helps strengthen the muscles in the fingers and firm up our fingertips. This type of practice is extremely beneficial when applied to scales and arpeggios.

Below is a D Major scale played two octaves in parallel motion.

Example 5j

The following exercises combine staccato playing with displaced rhythm applied to practicing scales.

In Example 5k, use a strong staccato so that the finger quickly strikes the key with force and pulls inward towards the palm of the hand. After striking each note, it is important to immediately let go of any tension in the hand and fingers.

When you play away from the center of the keyboard (RH ascending and LH descending) keep your hand at about a 45-degree angle to the keyboard. When the hands return to the center (RH descending and LH ascending), position your hands and wrists so that they run parallel to the keys on the piano.

Set the metronome to 60bpm and play the scale ascending and descending in each hand separately.

Example 5k

Now practice moving quickly from note to note by using a displaced rhythm. We will play this scale staccato by using the two different dotted 1/8th note patterns. Set the metronome so that the 1/4 note is equal to 40bpm.

I suggest working hands separately as we did in the previous examples. Remember that it is important to relax after each dotted 1/8th note. As we did with the previous example, remember how your hand, arm and forearm should be positioned when moving away from the center of the keyboard.

Example 5l

Now we will flip the rhythms around so that we begin with the 1/16th note instead of the dotted 1/8th. This changes the two-note combinations. The goal is to play the notes in quick succession, two at a time. The shorter note should "snap" into the longer ones. Listen to the audio to hear how it's done.

Example 5m

Now, set the metronome so that the 1/4 note is equal to 60bpm and play as written in Example 5j.

Arpeggios

Now let's apply the same process to arpeggios. Keep in mind that the thumb travels a greater distance under the fingers when playing arpeggios, so when you play an ascending arpeggio in the right hand or a descending arpeggio in the left, you will find that angling the hand, wrist and forearm away from the body is extremely helpful. The arm should glide across the keyboard and the elbow should not jerk up and down.

Use your arms and do not depend solely on the fingers. Focus on evenness of tone and don't concern yourself with connecting the notes smoothly because these examples are not marked legato. Ensure all the notes have equal volume and length, and that none are accented.

Below we have a D Major arpeggio played in two octaves

Example 5n

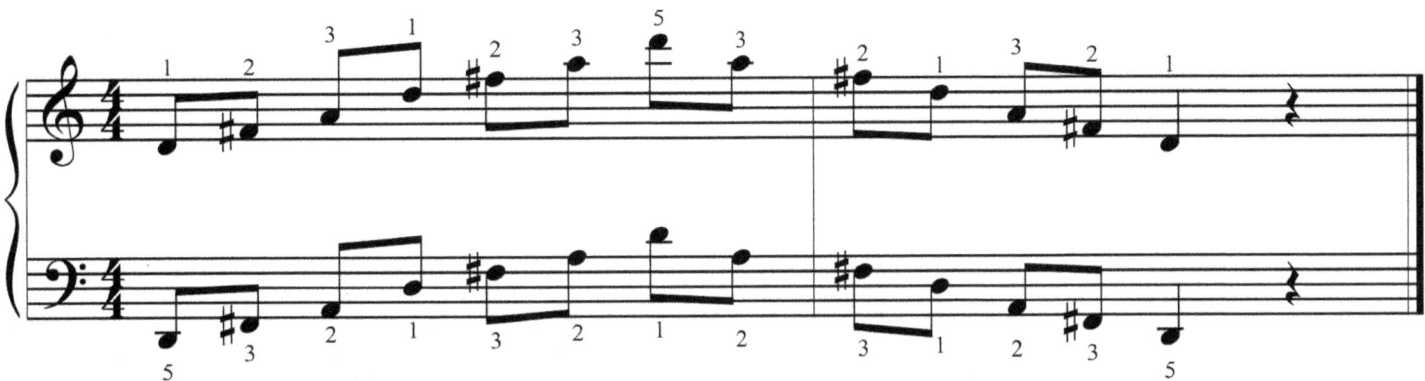

Set the metronome to 60bpm and play Example 5o ascending and descending in each hand separately (not hands together). Remember to use a strong staccato touch.

Example 5o

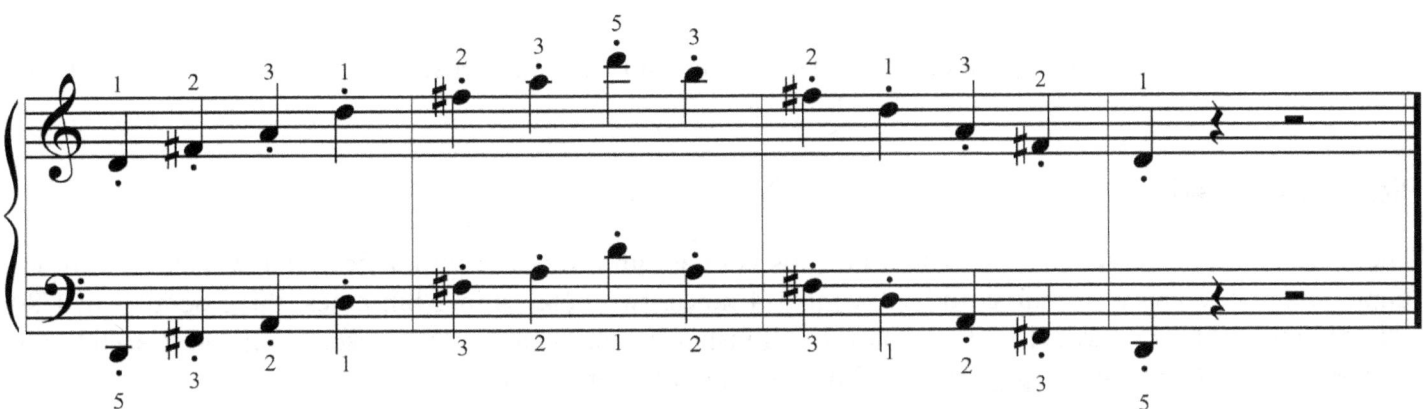

Next, play the arpeggio staccato with a displaced rhythm at 40bpm.

Example 5p

Now flip the rhythms around so that we begin with the 1/16th note instead of the dotted 1/8th. This changes the two-note combinations.

Example 5q

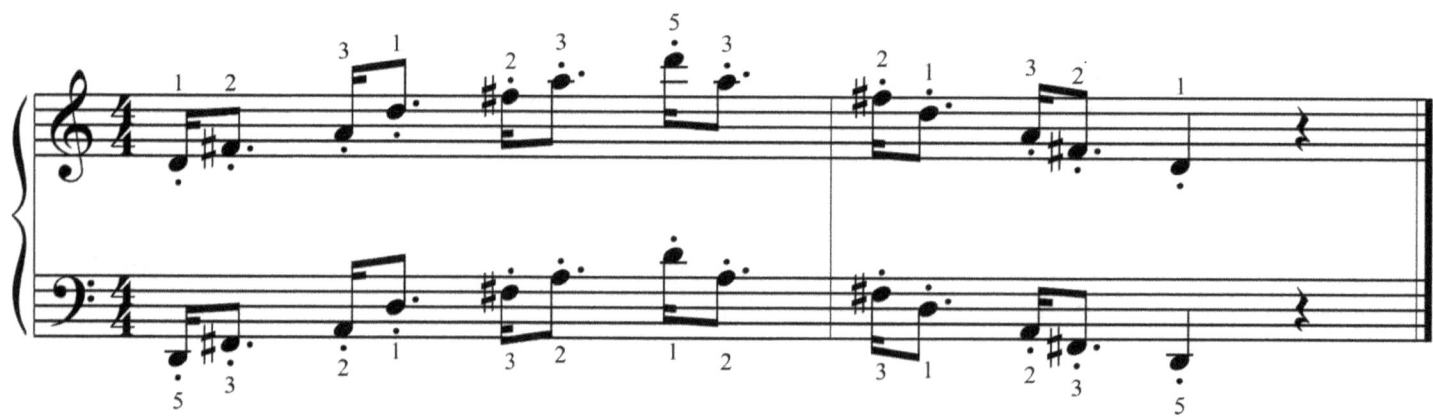

You can apply these ideas to any scale, arpeggio or passage of music that consists of a rapid succession of notes.

Picking Up Speed

One creative way to practice scales and arpeggios is to assign different rhythms to different octaves. For example, ascending and descending one octave in 1/4 notes, two octaves in 1/8th notes, three octaves in 1/8th note triplets and four octaves in 1/16th notes. In all instances, the scale is played ascending and descending in parallel motion. The related arpeggio should be played in the same manner

This exercise is a great way to warm up. If one of the pieces you are learning is in the key of A Major, you can warm up with the A Major scale and arpeggio in this way. The 1/16th notes control the maximum speed of the exercise so, if you can play the 1/16th notes comfortably at 60bpm, ensure you begin with the 1/4 notes at that speed.

If you're having trouble playing any scale or arpeggio at a particular tempo, especially over more than one octave, slow down and find a tempo that is manageable, even if it is very slow. From here, you can begin to increase the metronome speed in small increments until you've trained your fingers enough to hit your target speed. Be patient with yourself.

Note: When playing three or four notes per beat with a faster tempo there is not enough time to deliberately lift the fingers as we discussed earlier. Because your fingers are moving faster, you must lighten your touch so that you can play with fluidity. When it comes to speed, *lighter* equals *faster*.

Make sure you lean in the direction that you are playing. This is especially important when playing scales and arpeggios in three or four octaves because your hands are moving a great distance across the keyboard.

Summary of Practice Tips

Let's recap all the important things we've discussed in this chapter with regard to practicing scales and arpeggios. Firstly, know the fingering. This extremely important because knowing the correct fingering makes for better playing.

Also, allow for mobility of the thumb. How do we do this? We remember to angle our hand, wrist and forearm away from the body whenever we play away from the center of the piano (RH ascending and LH hand descending). Always remember to practice slowly with raised fingers, and also to practice staccato with displaced rhythm.

Practice with a metronome and as your playing improves at one speed, gradually take the tempo up a notch. Remember also to not always practice hands together. Work with each hand individually as well.

Chapter Six – Double Notes

Regardless of what genre of music you play you will often encounter double notes. Double notes are pairs of notes that sound together simultaneously. Here is an example of double notes played in thirds.

Example 6a

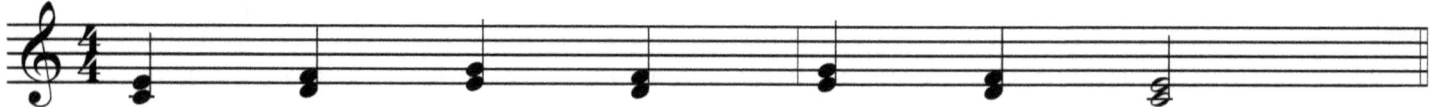

Double notes can occur in any interval, but the most common ones are thirds, sixths and octaves.

Thirds and sixths add harmonic support to a melody, while octaves add volume and fullness or reinforce the bass line. While one can go on at length on the topic of double notes, this chapter simply serves as an introduction to how one should approach playing them.

When playing double notes, the fingers work together in pairs. The first, second, and third fingers are strongest, and the fourth and fifth are weaker. In many cases, a note pair will consist of a strong finger and weak finger. For example, you may play a third with fingers 3 and 5, or a sixth with fingers 2 and 5. The goal is for both fingers to learn to sound the notes simultaneously with equal strength and speed.

Double Thirds

Double thirds are a good place to start when learning double notes. They are a short distance apart, so the hand is in more of a closed position and doesn't require any stretching.

Example 6b is a pattern in double thirds to play both staccato and legato.

Here are a couple helpful tips to remember:

1. Allow the wrist to maintain flexibility and to move from side to side, not to become locked or stuck in one position.

2. Keep the forearm and wrist aligned with the pair of notes you are playing.

3. Practice each hand separately, both legato and staccato. When playing staccato, remember to pull the fingers inward towards the palm of your hand. It doesn't need to be forceful like in previous chapters.

4. Practice in different keys. Learn the pattern in the original key of C Major then transpose it to the different easy major keys as part of your warm-up.

5. More experienced players can play the exercise ascending in half-steps through all 12 keys.

Example 6b

Here's one way you can play the exercise through each of the major keys.

Example 6c

If you can't play the pattern in all 12 major keys, transpose it to the ones you do know. For example, you could simply play the exercise in C, D, E, F, G, A and B.

Practice this exercise at a slow tempo – set your metronome at 60bpm and play one pair of notes per beat.

A Note About Playing Double Thirds Legato

Sometimes double thirds require fingers to cross over each other, and if you are a more experienced player you may run into these situations.

Example 6d shows the right hand playing a scale-like figure in double thirds.

You may find a legato passage similar to this in one of your piano pieces which requires fingers to cross over other fingers, but how do we play all the notes smoothly?

View the double notes as two individual voices but know that it may not always be possible to play both pairs of notes smoothly. In the bottom voice, you will need to slide the finger across first two notes to create the illusion of legato in beats 1 and 2.

It is not possible to connect the F in the last beat to the G on the first beat in the following measure. This is because the first and third fingers need to cross over the other fingers. However, if you look at the notes in the top voice (A and B), the A can be held down by the fifth finger until the next pair of notes (G and B) are played by the first and third fingers.

In these instances, aim to join one of the notes in the pair, preferably the upper voice whenever possible because it usually carries the melody.

Example 6d

A powerful way to practice thirds is to play the top voice legato and the bottom voice staccato. This will help clarify the notes in the melody. You may wish to practice the top voice in isolation, but if you do this, ensure that you use the same fingering as when playing both voices together.

When it comes to double notes, fingering is crucial. Decide on a good fingering and stick with it. Often sheet music will have fingerings written in for you, but if not, you can always consult different sources to help you decide what to use. Such sources include *The Virtuoso Pianist in 60 Exercises* by Hanon and *School of Scales and Double Notes for the Pianoforte, Op. 64* by Moritz Moszkowski (1854–1925).

Double Sixths

Examples 6e and 6f are ascending and descending double sixths exercises based on a four-note pattern. Newer players should focus on just Example 6e until your skills have advanced.

Before you study Example 6e, look at examples 6g and 6h to learn how you should practice this technique.

Example 6e

Example 6f

Let's work through the practice tips we learned for playing double thirds by using Example 6e as a model.

We will begin with the right hand first.

Isolate the notes in the upper voice and play them legato using the same fingering as if you were playing both voices together.

Example 6g

Next, play the top voice legato while playing the bottom voice staccato. Keep the lower voice slightly softer than the bottom voice because the melody is often carried by the upper voice. Learning to keep the lower voice quieter will help preserve the dynamics.

Example 6h

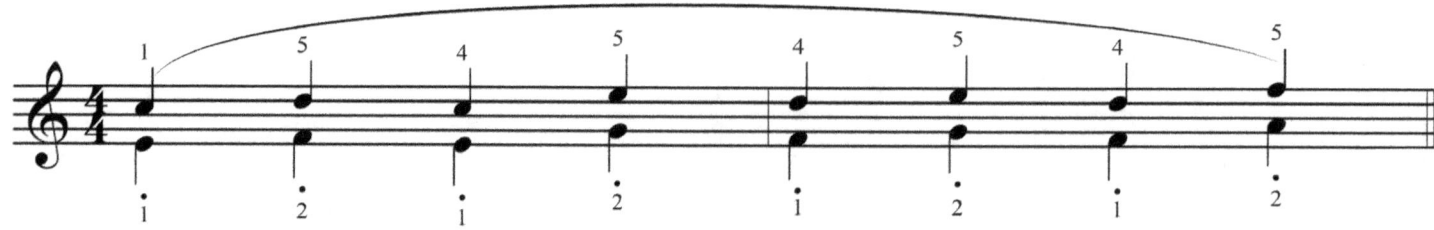

Now play Example 6e as written and try to lean a little more on the upper voice.

If you are a beginner, or just find it too much of a stretch to play these exercises, you can modify the fingering of these examples. For example, in the right hand you could use the fingering below – just remember to slide the thumb to help the lower voice to sound more legato.

Even if you are unable to achieve a smooth legato in both voices, be sure that at least one voice is legato. In this example, that would be the top voice.

Example 6i

Note: Music that calls for the use of the pedal can also help you create the illusion of legato when playing a passage that contains double sixths.

Practice the Example 6e slowly at 60bpm with your right hand, playing one note to the beat. Practice it legato as well as staccato. When playing staccato, you can play all the pairs using fingers 1 and 5 for ease. Remember to immediately relax after playing a note pair to prevent any build up of tension.

Use the following three steps to practice this kind of example:

1. Play the isolated upper voice legato using the same fingering as if it was paired.

2. Play the top voice legato while playing the bottom voice staccato.

3. Play the exercises legato as written.

4. Play the exercises staccato using fingers 1 and 5.

Once you have played through these steps with your right hand, use the same approach with your left. Your hands are mirror images of each other, so when playing with the left hand, the 1st and 2nd fingers play the notes in the upper voice and the 4th and 5th fingers play the notes in the lower voice. You will find it easier to bring out the melody in the upper voice because the 1st and 2nd fingers are naturally stronger.

Sixths as a Prerequisite to Playing Octaves

The best way to learn octaves is to practice the technique on a smaller interval. Because they are so pleasing to the ear, we will use sixths which have the same type of movement. Because sixths are not as wide an interval as octaves, we can better learn this technique without worrying about overstretching the hands.

Example 6j shows the scale of C Major in double 6ths played with fingers 1 and 5.

Unlike the previous exercises the fingering is the same throughout and there is no need to worry about playing legato.

Using your right hand, play the first note pair, E and C, a few times. Notice how your hand feels when you relax and allow gravity to take over.

To play the sixth, lift your hand and allow it to drop down onto the keyboard freely, using the natural weight of your arm. It should fall freely in one continuous motion onto the keys.

However, you must maintain a solid hand shape with firm fingertips so that you can freely move from sixth to sixth accurately, and the hand should not be completely relaxed when it falls onto the keys. It's not a "flop" but a "drop"! The wrist and the muscles in the forearm should be loose while the hand should be firm but not tense. Your fingers should remain relatively close to the keys – you don't need to drop down from high above the keyboard.

Move from one pair of notes to the next accurately, relaxing after each is played. Once you can do this comfortably with sixths the technique will transfer directly to your octave playing.

It is important to relax after playing each pair of notes because this prevents tension from building up as you move to the next pair of notes.

When you're comfortable with this movement, practice the whole exercise no quicker than 60bpm.

Follow the same approach for the left hand.

Example 6j

Octaves

The most common fingering for octaves is 1 and 5 on white keys, and 1 and 4 on black keys. However, if you are a pianist with small hands, I suggest using 1 and 5 on all octaves as it will prevent your hand from over stretching and this is perfectly fine in all cases.

Let's apply what we learned when playing sixths to playing right hand octaves in Example 6k.

1. Lift your hand and allow your hand to drop down onto the keyboard freely, using the natural weight of the arm.

2. Maintain the same hand shape so you can freely move from one octave pair to the next while keeping the muscles in the wrist and forearm relaxed.

3. **Focus on accuracy and relaxing after each playing each pair!**

4. Practice at a speed no quicker than 60bpm.

5. Follow the same approach for the left hand.

Example 6k

If you have small hands, here are a couple of suggestions you can use to build strength and reach.

Practice the notes in the upper voice with the fifth finger alone to improve strength and accuracy.

Example 6l

Try to use more weight on the 5th finger than the 1st. The thumb is larger and stronger than the pinky and requires less effort to play. By focusing more weight on the 5th finger, both voices are more likely to sound together. This is best applied to pieces with lighter octave playing, especially if they are working as a left hand bass accompaniment.

Note: If you are playing a composition in which the left hand plays the melody in octaves while the right hand plays a softer accompaniment, it is fine to naturally allow more weight to fall to the thumb as you are simply highlighting the melody.

When you practice Example 6l in other keys you will be playing octaves on black notes, and it is perfectly fine to use fingers 1 and 5 for these octaves too. If you play an exercise or passage that contains both white and black-key octaves, keep your fingers as close to the black keys as possible to allow your hand to move in a straight line across the keys for more efficient playing. If you play the white key octaves to close to the edge of the keyboard, it will force your hand to move forwards and back to play the black keys.

Application

Let's take everything that we have learned in this chapter and apply it to some real melodies. The following examples are melodies taken from classical music.

The melody below is taken from the theme of Johann Pachelbel's *Canon in D Major.*

Example 6m

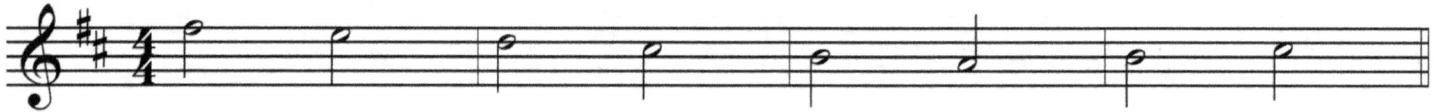

Play the example as written to gather a sense of what it sounds like. Take note of the key signature. It has two sharps (F and C are played as F♯ and C♯).

Then add a third *below* the notes by skipping over one letter name. In this case, the first pair of notes you will play in the first measure will be F♯ and D.

Continue to play the melody in thirds.

Based on what we discussed in this chapter on double thirds, see if you can work on a good fingering to use.

The next melody is a portion of the traditional hymn, *Amazing Grace.*

Example 6n

Play the example as written to gather a sense of what it sounds like.

Now add a sixth below the notes by skipping over four white notes on the keyboard. The first pair of notes you will play in the first measure will be G and B.

Continue to play the melody in sixths.

Based on what we discussed in this chapter on double sixths, see if you can work on a good fingering to use that is comfortable for you.

The final melody is taken from the final movement from Wolfgang Amadeus Mozart's *Piano Sonata No. 11 in A, K331/ 300i,* which is better known as *Rondo alla Turca.*

Example 6o

Play the example as written to gather a sense of what it sounds like. Notice the key signature has three sharps (F♯, C♯ and G♯).

Play the melody in octaves, remembering to maintain the same hand shape, allowing yourself to freely move from one octave to the next while keeping the muscles in the wrist and forearm relaxed.

Move from one pair of notes to the next accurately, relaxing after playing each one.

Chapter Seven – Major Scales

Learning the 12 major scales can seem like a daunting task. How do we remember all those fingerings?! This chapter helps you easily learn the scale fingerings by placing the twelve major scales into different groups based on their common fingering characteristics.

Note: It is not necessary to learn the scales in the order that they are presented here. As mentioned in Chapter Five, you may find it easier to start with the B Major scale as it fits nicely under the hand.

C Major Scale Fingering

We will first look at the C Major scale fingering.

R.H. 1 2 3 1 2 3 4 5 (subsume 1 for 5 if continuing to play the next octave)

L.H. 5 4 3 2 1 3 2 1

The example below shows the fingering used for an ascending and descending C Major scale played in two octaves.

Example 7a

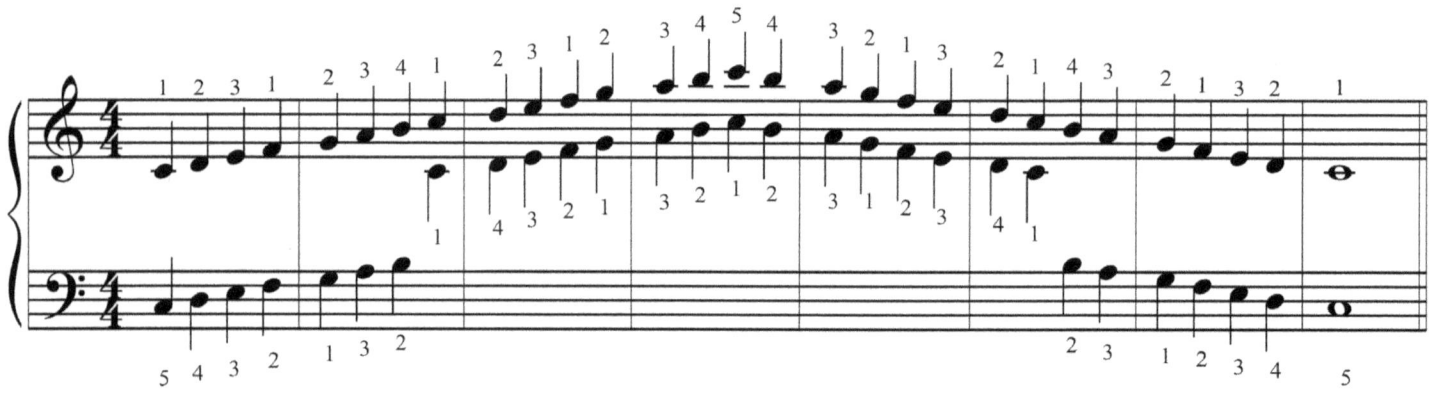

This C Major scale fingering is also used to play four other major scales:

- G Major
- D Major
- A Major
- E Major

These are shown in the following examples.

Pay close attention to the key signatures so you know which notes are played sharp.

Example 7b

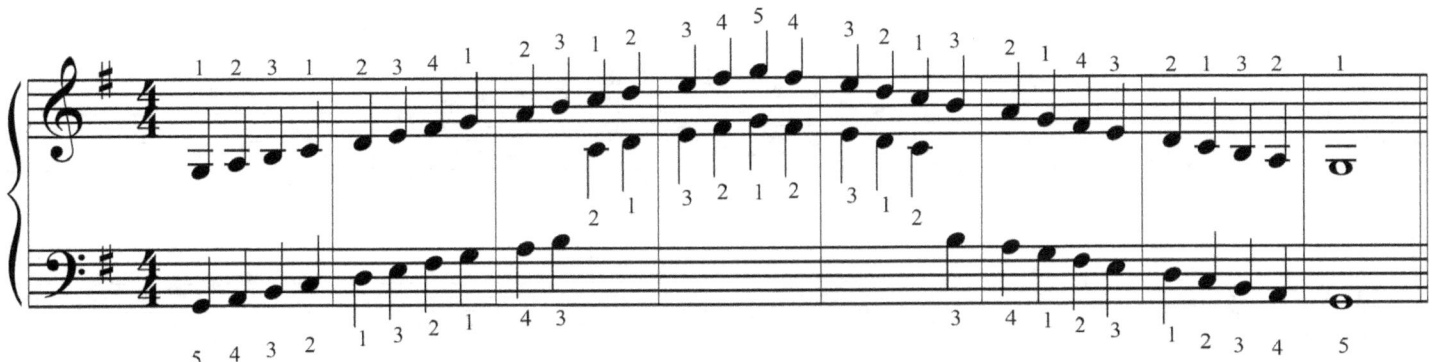

Example 7c

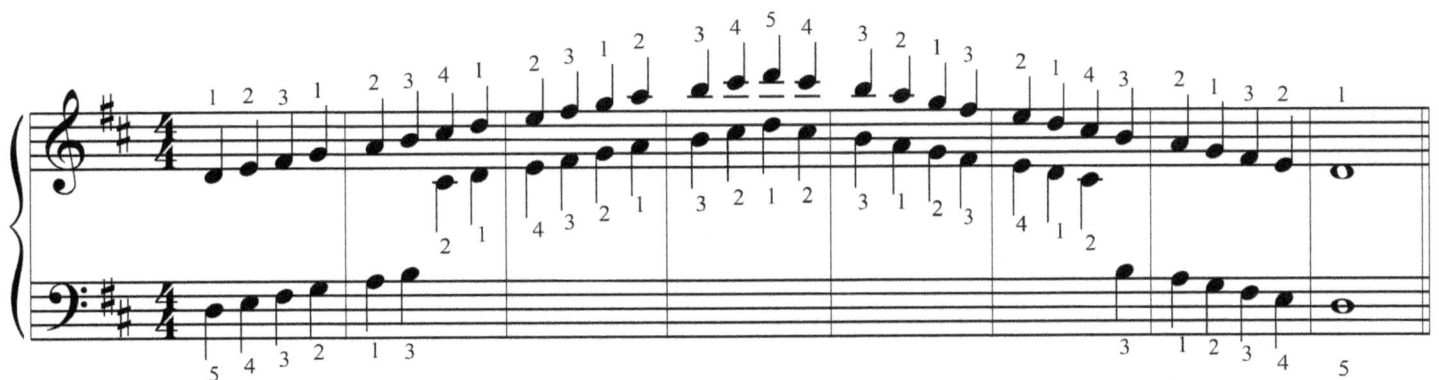

Example 7d

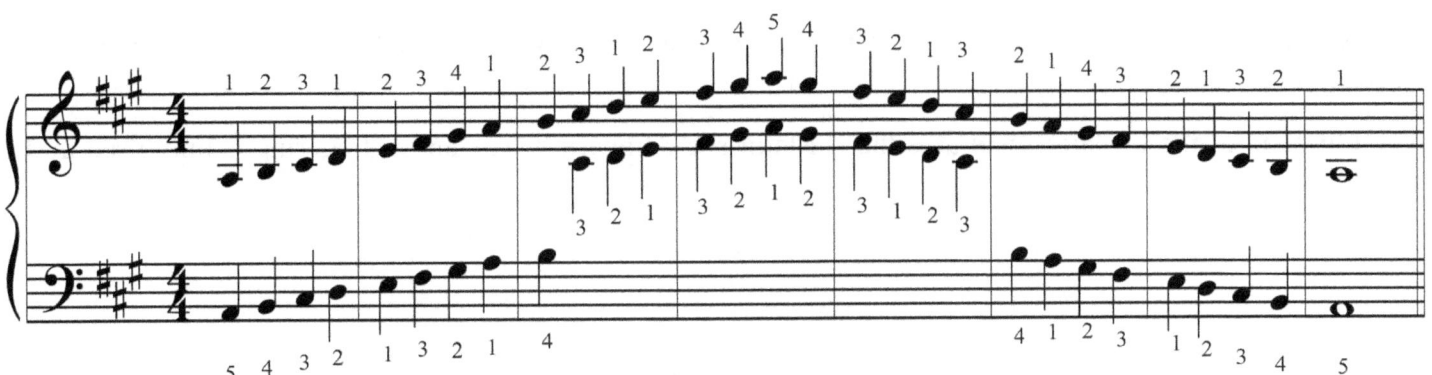

Example 7e

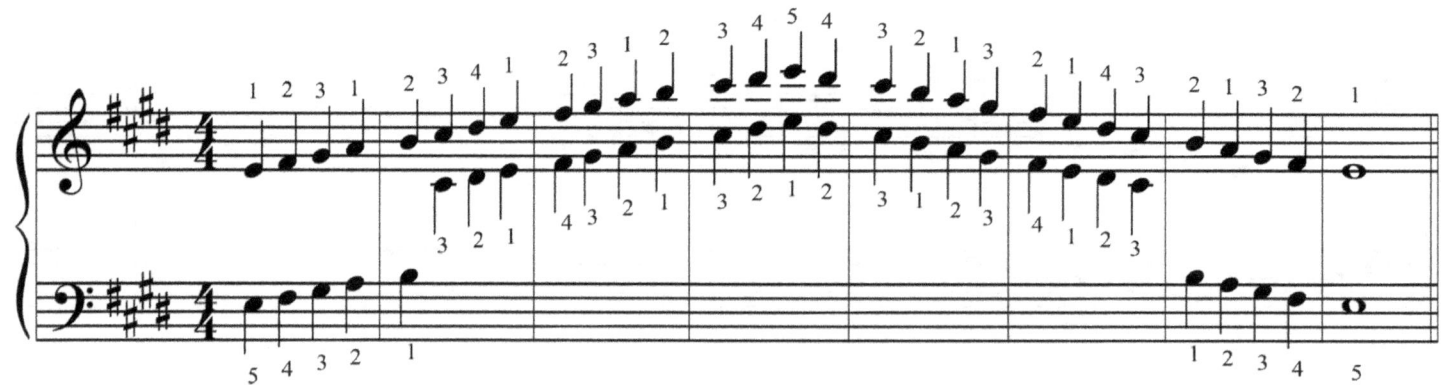

Major Scales that do not use the C Major fingering

The next group of four major scales consist of

- F Major
- B♭ Major
- E♭ Major
- A♭ Major

They all have the following fingering characteristics:

1. The 4th finger in the right hand always lands on a B♭.
2. The 4th finger of the left hand always lands on the fourth note of the scale.

The only exception to the second rule is in F Major where the 4th finger of the left hand lands on the second degree, G.

The left hand of the F Major scale uses the C Major scale fingering. The above fingering is only used in the right hand.

Example 7f

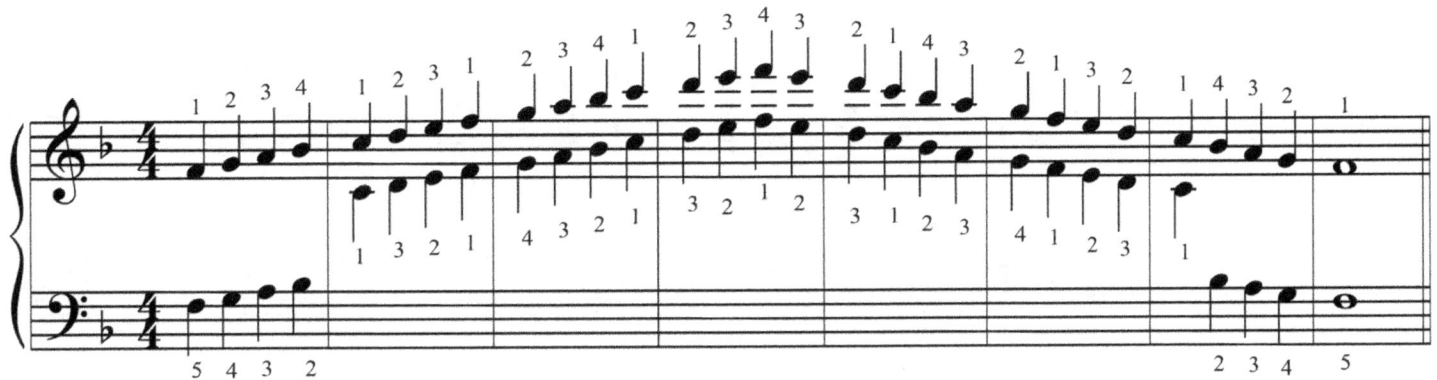

B♭ Major, E♭ Major and A♭ Major are shown in the following examples.

These scales begin on black keys, so the first note is not played with the thumb.

Example 7g

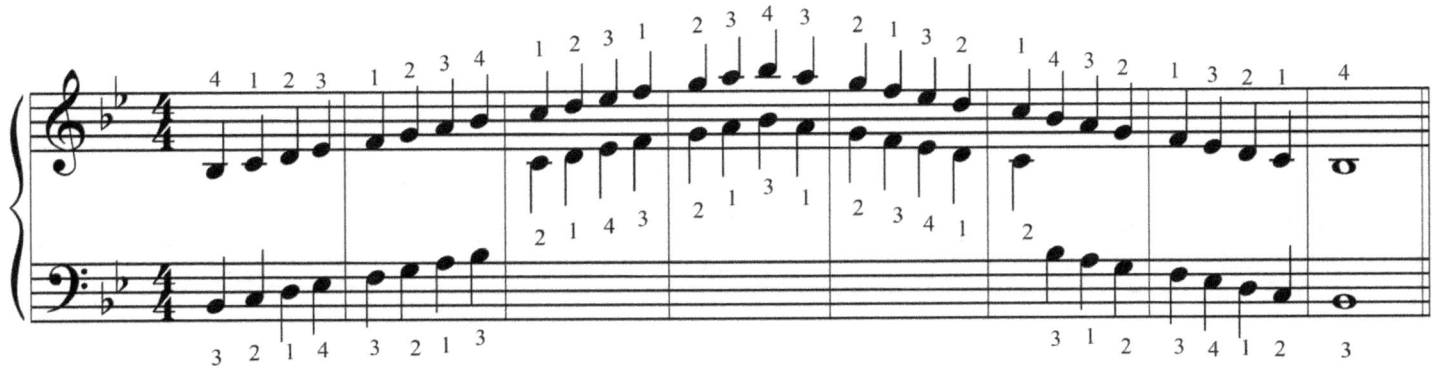

Example 7h

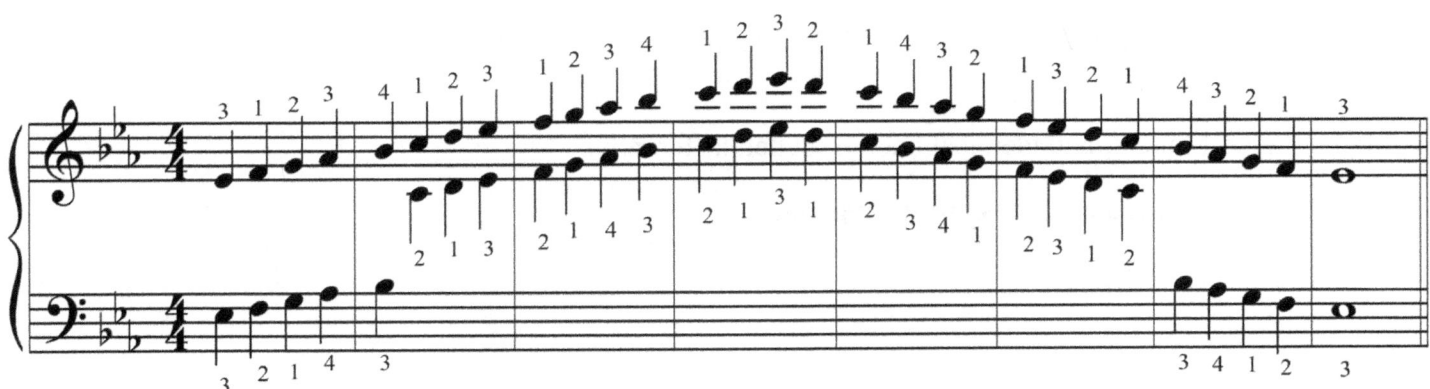

Example 7i

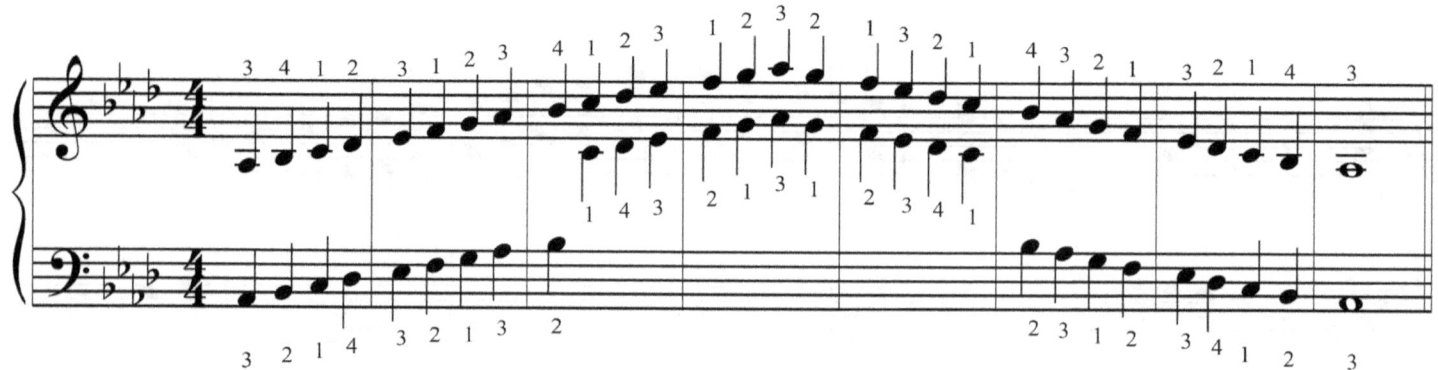

The following three major scales all contain groups of three and two black keys.

In these scales, fingers 2 and 3 play C♯ and D♯ (or D♭ and E♭) and fingers 2, 3 and 4 play F♯, G♯ and A♯ (or G♭, A♭ and B♭).

The example below shows the B Major scale. Notice that the right hand uses the C Major fingering. The difference in fingering lies in the left hand.

Example 7j

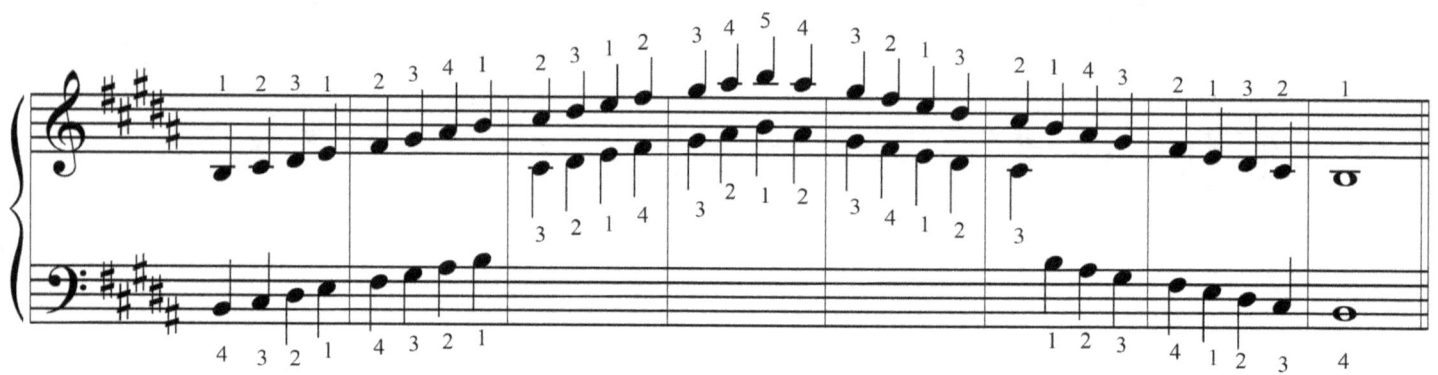

Note: The B Major scale sounds identical to C♭ Major. Its key signature has seven flats and consists of the notes C♭, D♭, E♭, F♭, G♭, A♭, B♭, C♭.

B Major and C♭ Major sound identical but are spelled differently.

Here is the D♭ Major scale with its proper fingering.

Example 7k

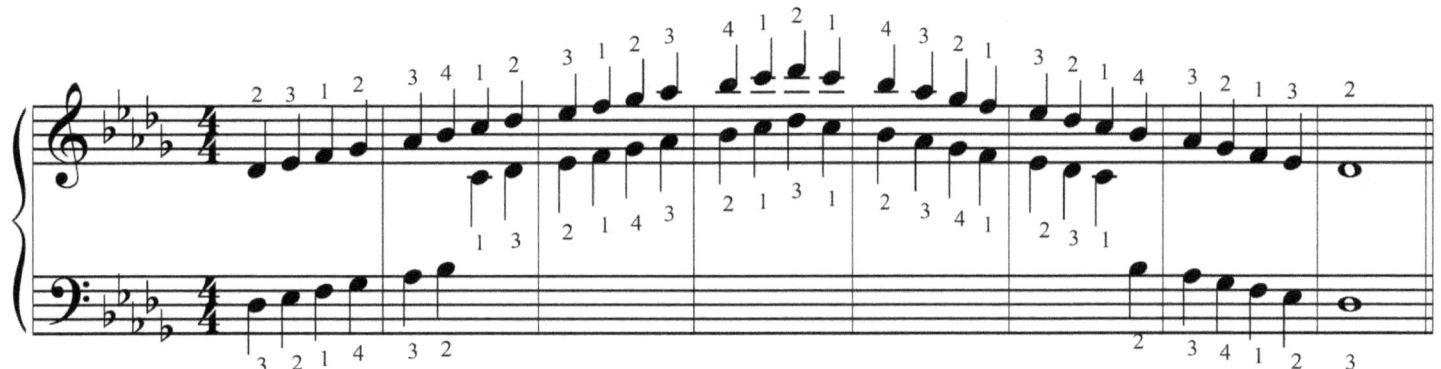

Note: The D♭ Major scale sounds identical to C♯ Major. The key signature for the C♯ Major scale contains 7 sharps and consists of the notes C♯, D♯, E♯, F♯, G♯, A♯, B♯, C♯.

Example 7l shows the G♭ Major scale with its proper fingering.

Example 7l

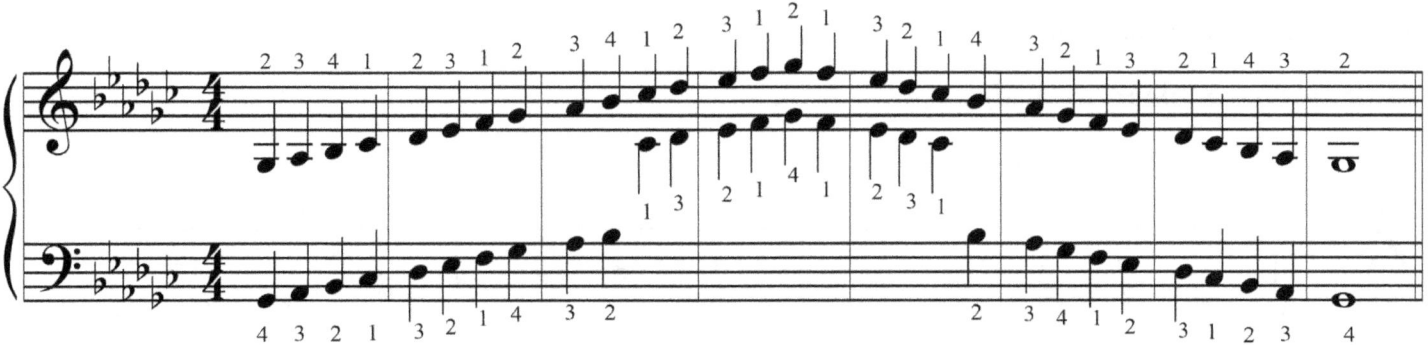

The G♭ Major scale can also be spelled as F♯ Major. This scale contains 6 sharps and is spelled F♯, G♯, A♯, B, C♯, D♯, E♯, F♯.

Chapter Eight – Minor Scales

Once you feel comfortable with major scales, you can begin studying your minor scales. Before we go over the fingerings, let's discuss a few things.

Unlike major scales, the minor scale has three forms: natural, harmonic and melodic.

Natural minor scales are built by starting on the 6th degree of their relative major scale. Below we have a C Major scale.

Example 8a

If we go to the 6th scale degree, we land on the note A. Because of this relationship, the key of A minor is called the *relative minor* of C Major. For every major scale, there is a relative minor scale and both scales have the same key signature. Notice that A minor and C Major have no sharps or flats in their key signatures.

Below is the A minor scale in its natural form. We call this the type of scale a natural minor because none of the notes in the scale are altered.

Example 8b – A minor (natural)

The harmonic minor scale has the same notes as the natural minor scale except that the 7th degree is raised a half step. Thus, G is played as G♯.

Example 8c – A minor (harmonic)

In the melodic minor scale, the 6th and 7th scale degrees are raised a half step ascending and lowered descending. Thus, F and G are played as F# and G# on the way up and then as F♮ and G♮ on the way back down.

Example 8d – A minor (melodic)

Minor Scales Organization

As with major scales, the minor scales are written to span two octaves. To save time, we will not go over all three forms of the minor scale in all 12 keys. Instead we focus on the harmonic minor scale as our model and the melodic and natural forms will only be given when there are exceptions to the fingering rules.

While I encourage you to at least become familiar with all three forms of the minor scale, it is not absolutely necessary to practice all three. If you must choose between one form to incorporate into your practice, I recommend the harmonic minor because of its unusual feel and due to the wider interval between the 6th and 7th degrees of the scale.

Scales that Use the C Major Fingering

Here are the five minor scales that use the C Major Scale fingering regardless of whether they are played as natural, harmonic or melodic forms.

- A minor
- D minor
- G minor
- C minor
- E minor

Pay attention to the key signatures so you know which notes are played sharp or flat.

Example 8e – A minor (harmonic)

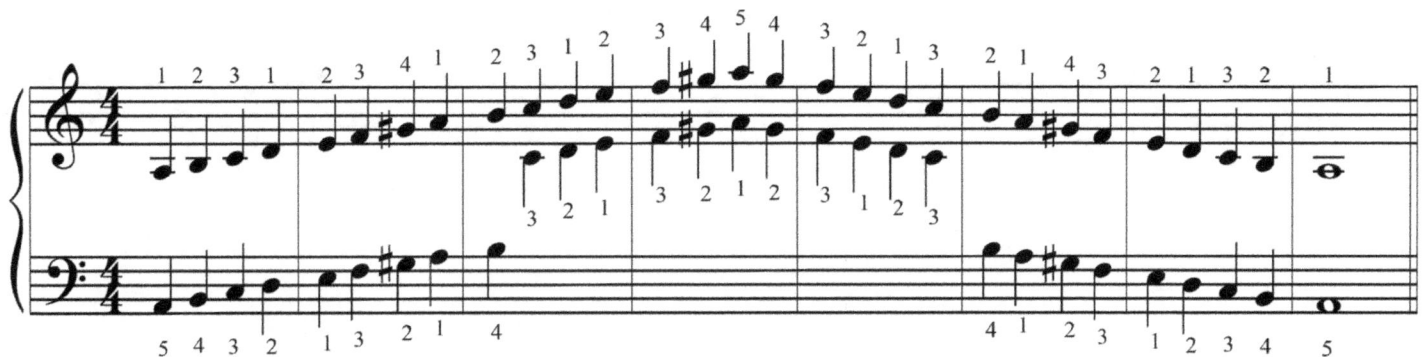

Example 8f – D minor (harmonic)

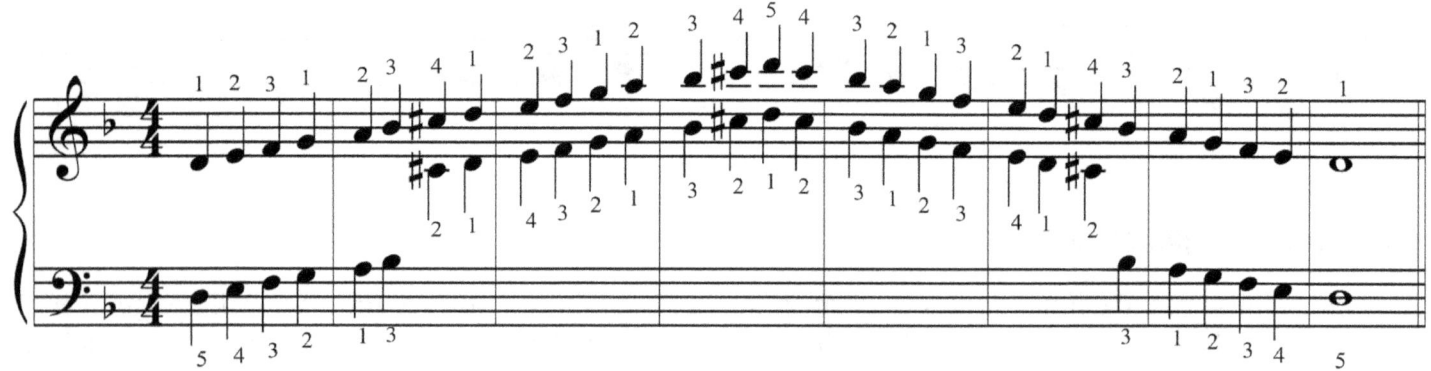

Example 8g – G minor (harmonic)

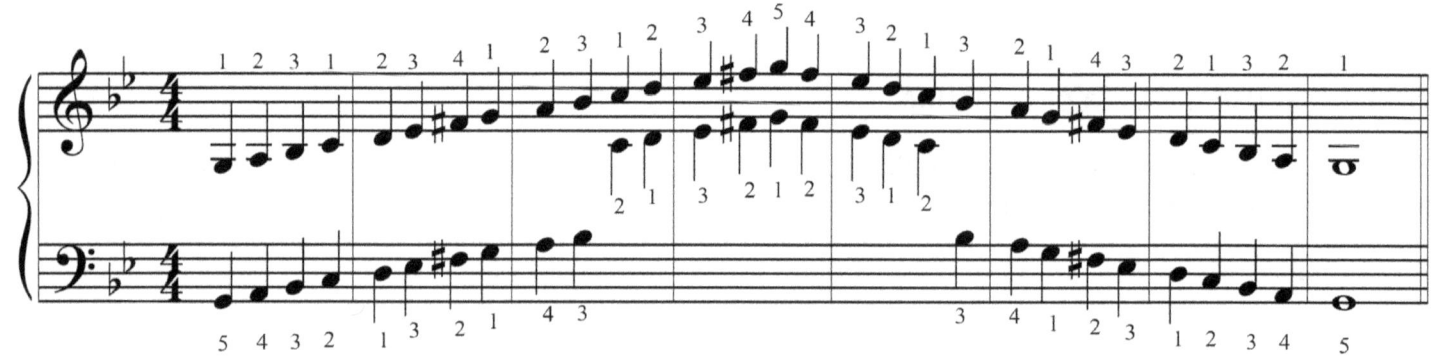

Example 8h – C minor (harmonic)

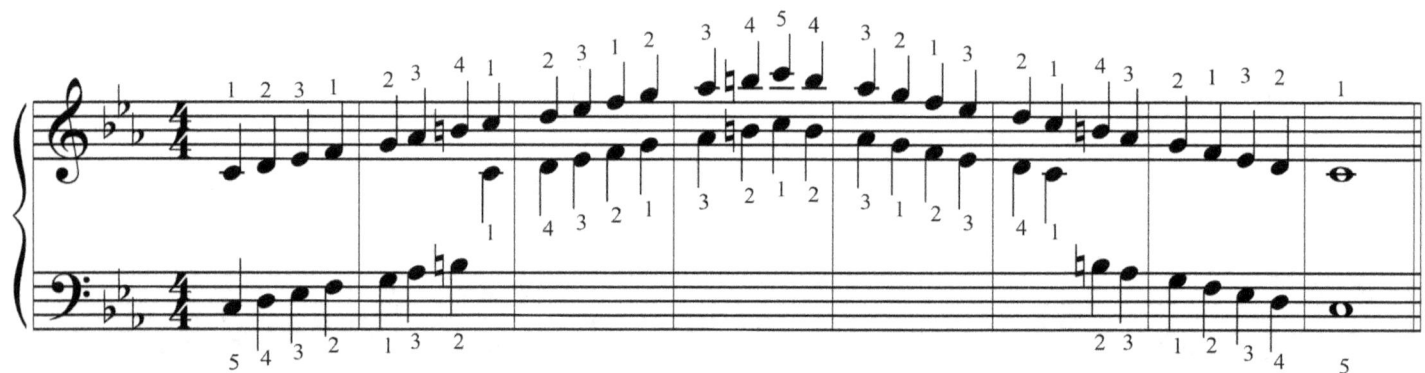

Example 8i – E minor (harmonic)

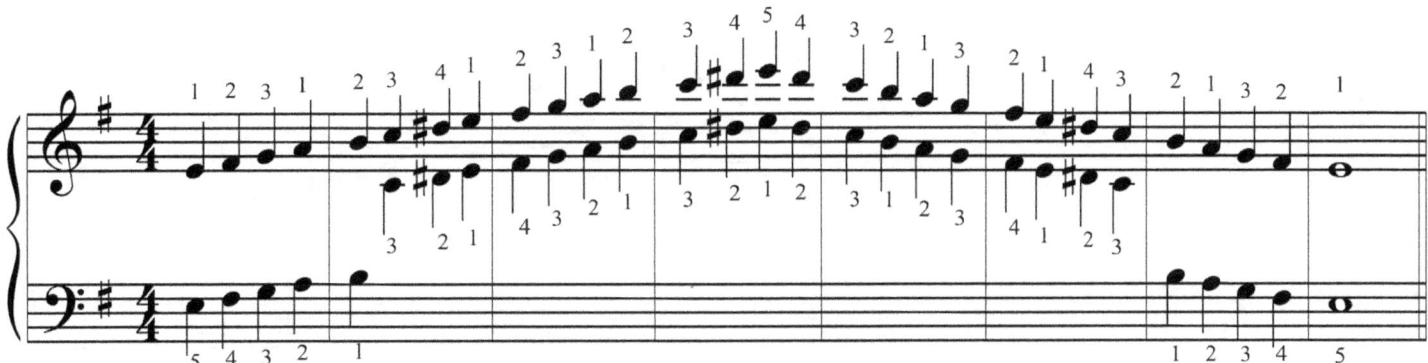

Note: To change the harmonic minor to a natural minor, simply lower the 7th scale degree. To change the harmonic minor to a melodic minor, raise the 6th degree ascending and then lower the 6th and 7th scale degrees descending.

F Minor and B Minor

Now we will discuss the minor scales that do not use the C Major fingerings in both hands.

The following scales use the same fingering patterns as their parallel majors. These fingering also work in all three forms of the minor scale.

The B minor scale uses the same fingering pattern as its parallel major (see B Major, Example 7j).

Example 8j – B minor (harmonic)

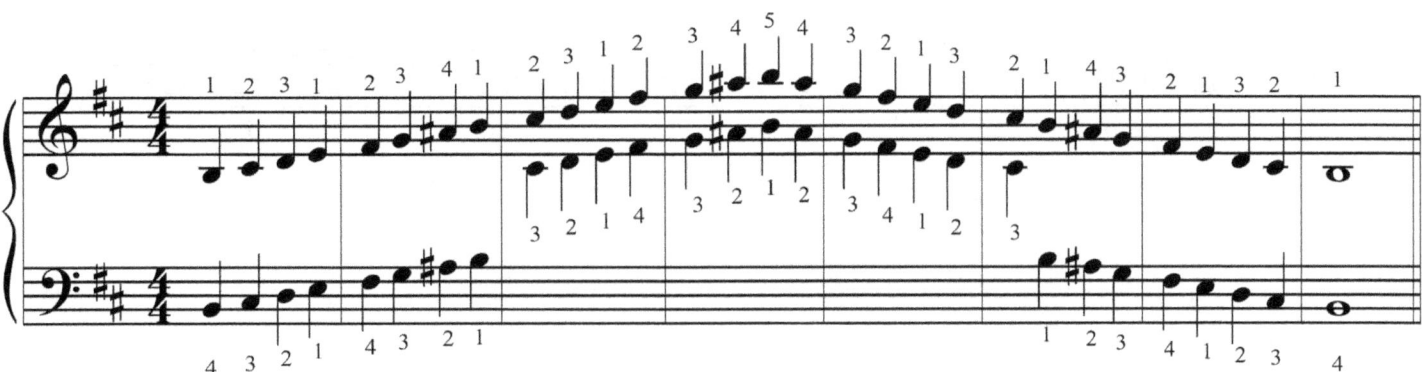

Likewise, The F minor scale uses the same fingering as F Major (see Example 7f)

Example 8k – F minor (harmonic)

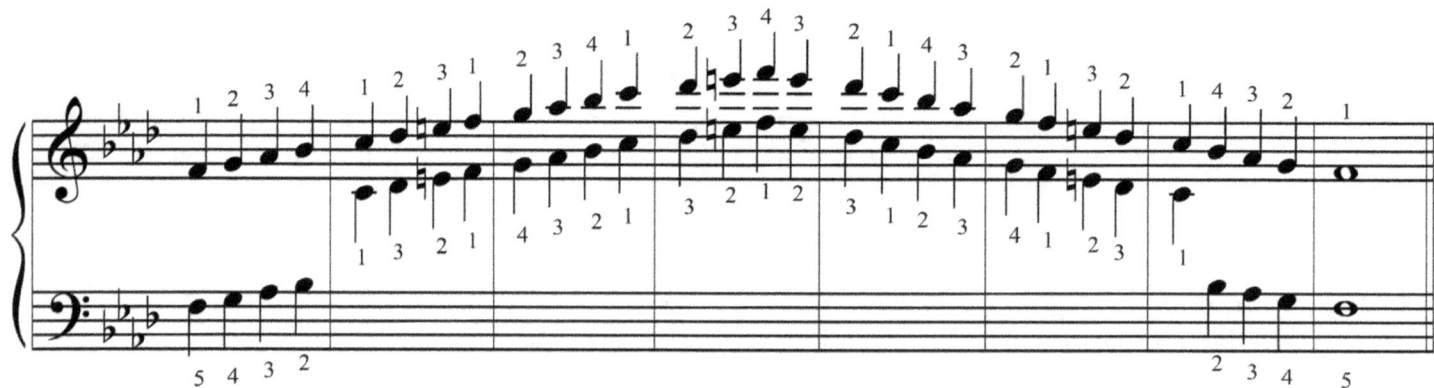

Exceptions to the Rule

Until now, all the minor scales presented use the same fingering as their parallel major scales. However, for the remaining minor scales, all characteristics do not hold true.

The same fingerings for B♭ and E♭ minor scales can be used for all three forms of the minor scale but the fingering patterns are unlike the B♭ and E♭ Major scales.

Example 8l – B♭ minor (harmonic)

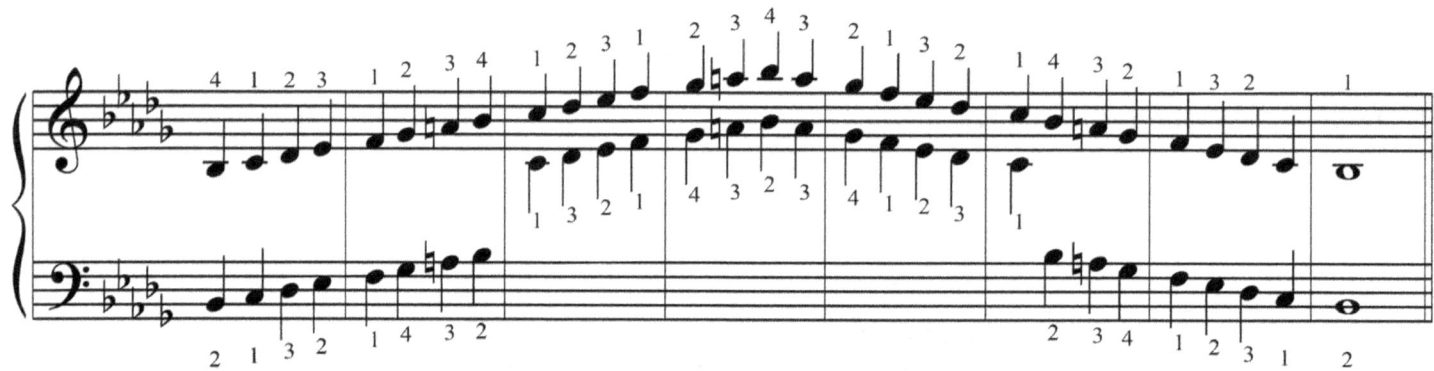

Example 8m – E♭ Minor (harmonic)

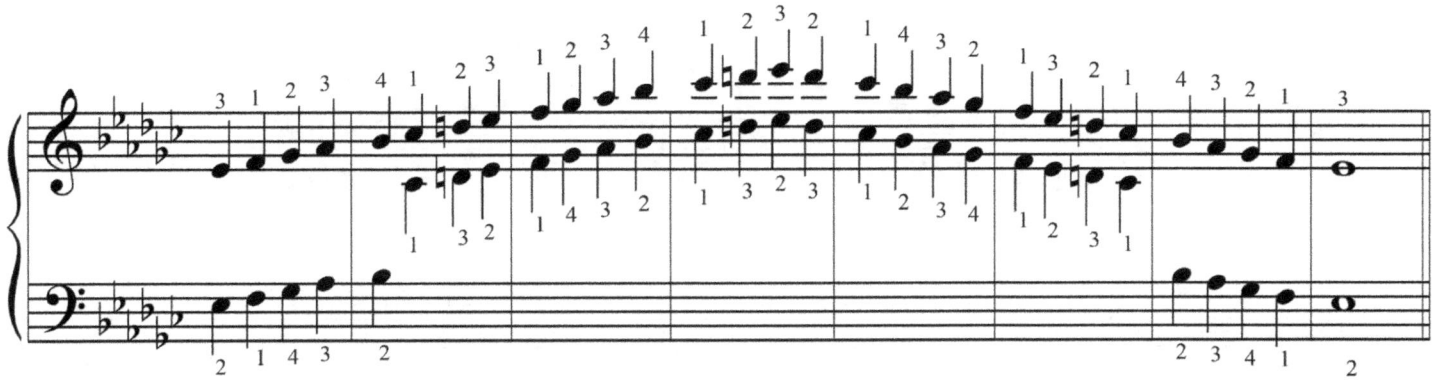

The F♯ harmonic and natural minors both use the following fingering.

R.H. 3 4 1 2 3 1 2 3

L.H. 4 3 2 1 3 2 1 3

In the example below notice that the fingering for the left hand is the same for the parallel major scale (see G♭ Major, Example 7l). The change in fingering is in the right hand only.

Example 8n – F♯ minor (harmonic)

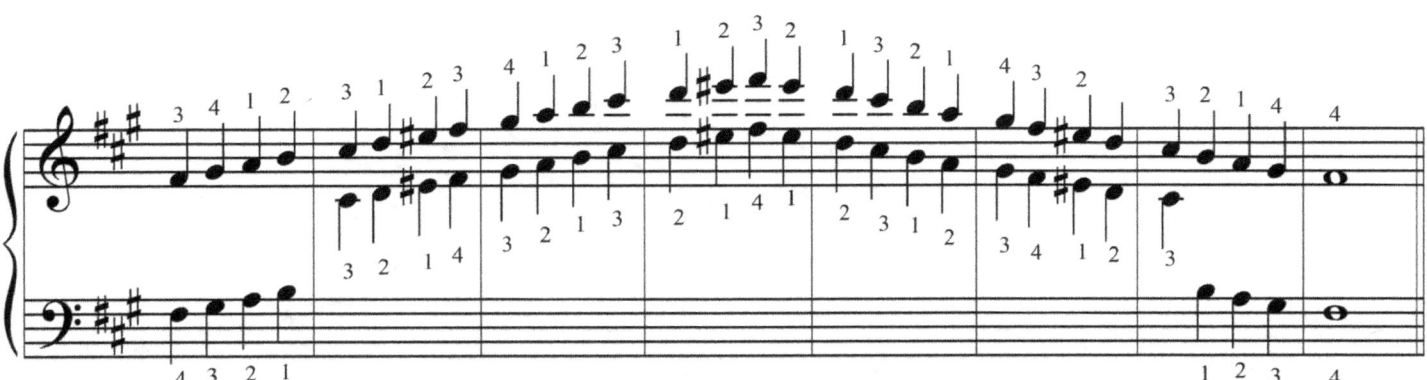

The F♯ melodic minor uses a different fingering pattern in the right hand from that of the harmonic minor. Notice also how the fingering changes when the scale descends. Again, the fingering in the left hand remains unchanged.

Example 8o – F♯ minor (melodic)

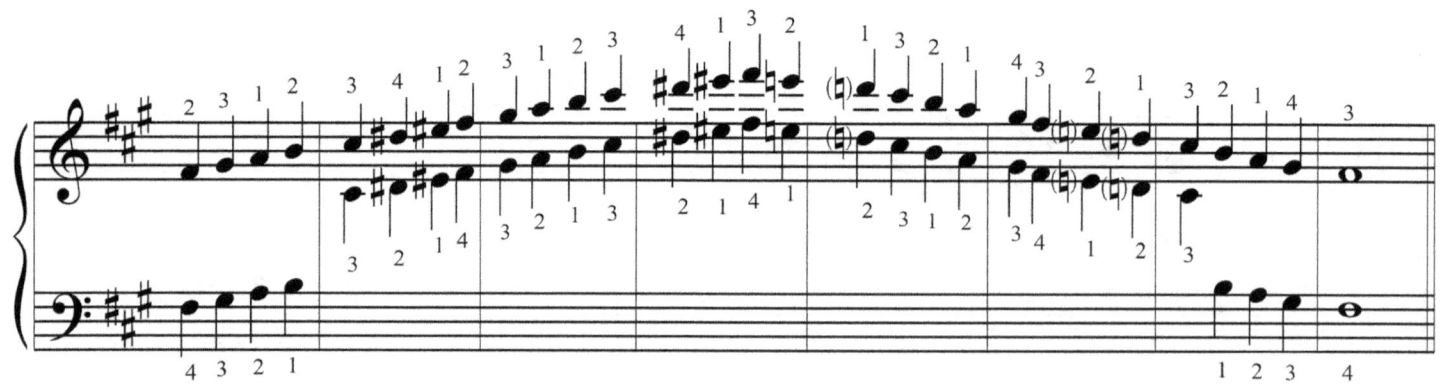

The following fingerings are used for the C♯ harmonic and natural minors. Again, the left hand uses the same fingering pattern as its parallel major (see D♭ Major, Example 7k)

R.H. 3 4 1 2 3 1 2 3

L.H. 3 2 1 4 3 2 1 3

The fingering for the left hand is the same for the parallel major (see D♭ Major, Example 7k). Also, notice that the right hand fingering pattern is the same as the C♯ minor harmonic scale (see Example 8n).

Example 8p

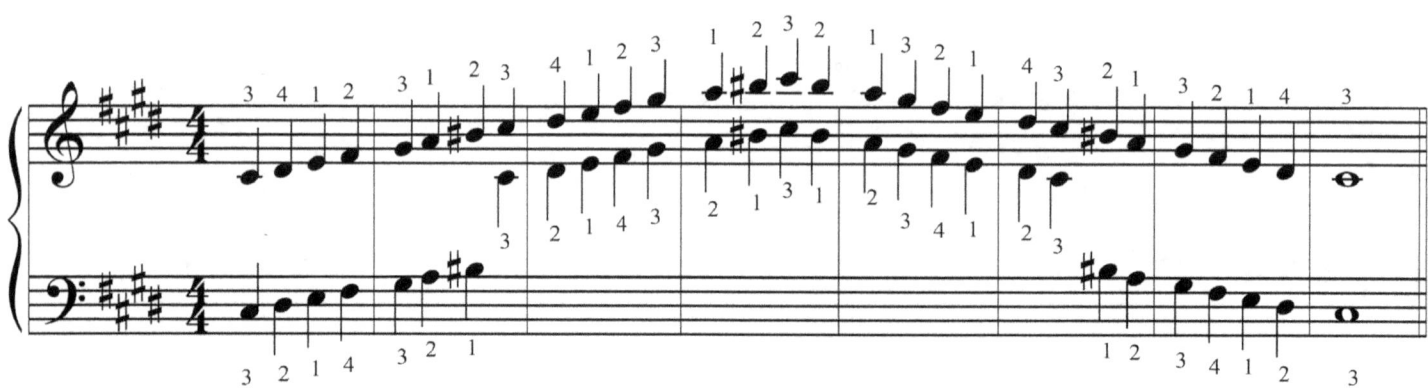

The C♯ melodic minor scale uses a different fingering pattern in the right hand. Likewise, the fingering also changes when the scale descends.

Example 8q

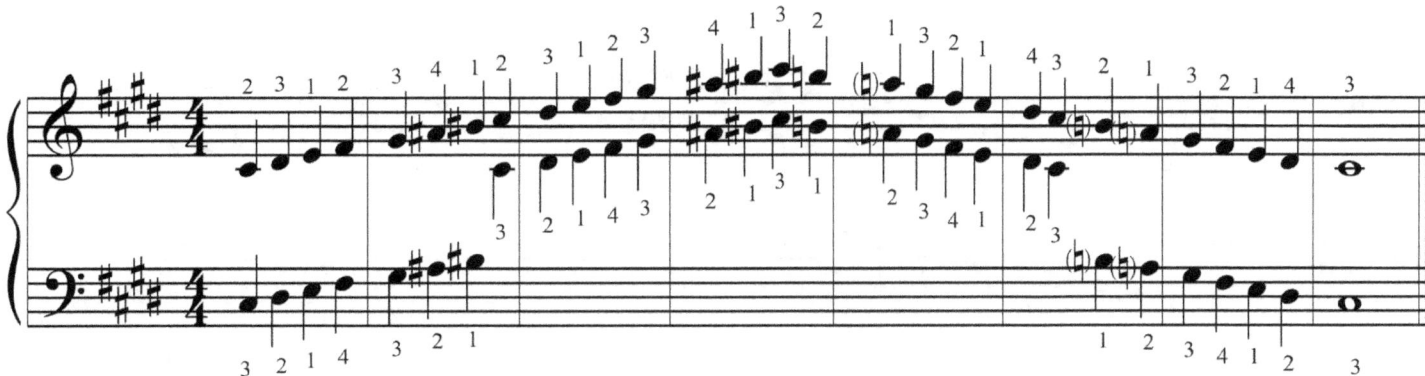

The G♯ minor harmonic scale uses the same fingering its parallel major scale (see A♭ Major, Example 7i).

Example 8r – G♯ minor (harmonic)

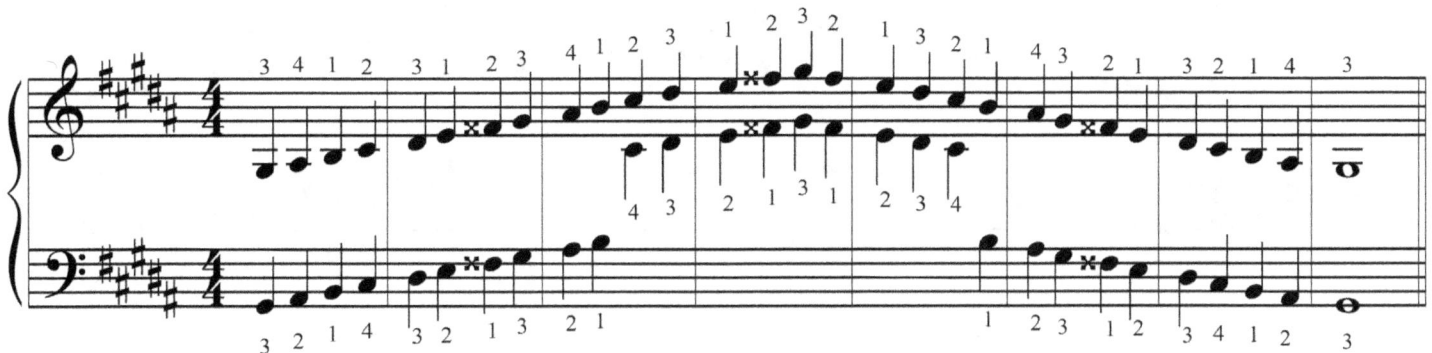

However, both the natural and melodic forms use different fingering patterns in the left hand.

Example 8s presents the G♯ minor scale in its melodic form with the change in the right hand fingering beginning when the scale descends. Example 8t presents in its natural form. The fingering in the right hand remains unchanged.

Example 8s – G♯ minor (melodic)

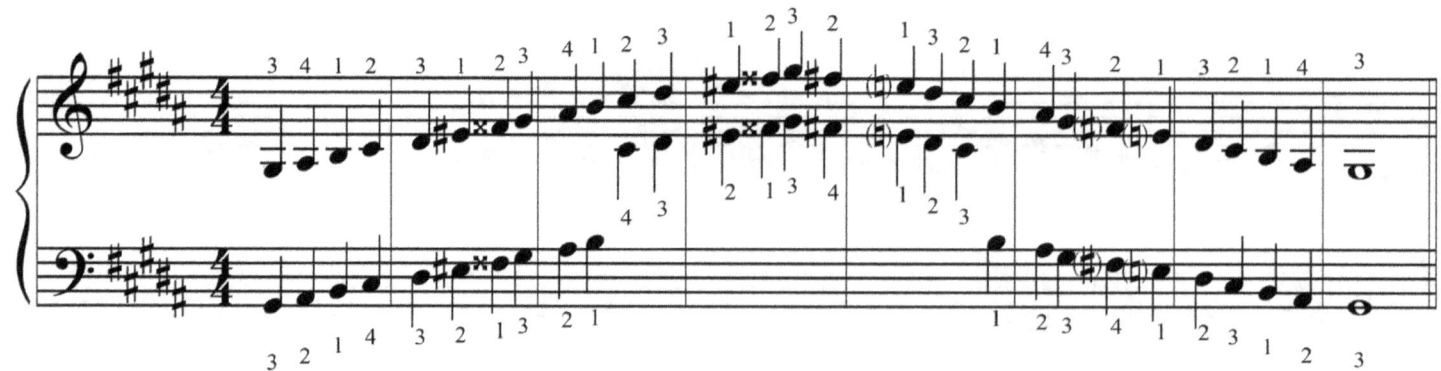

Example 8t – G♯ minor (natural)

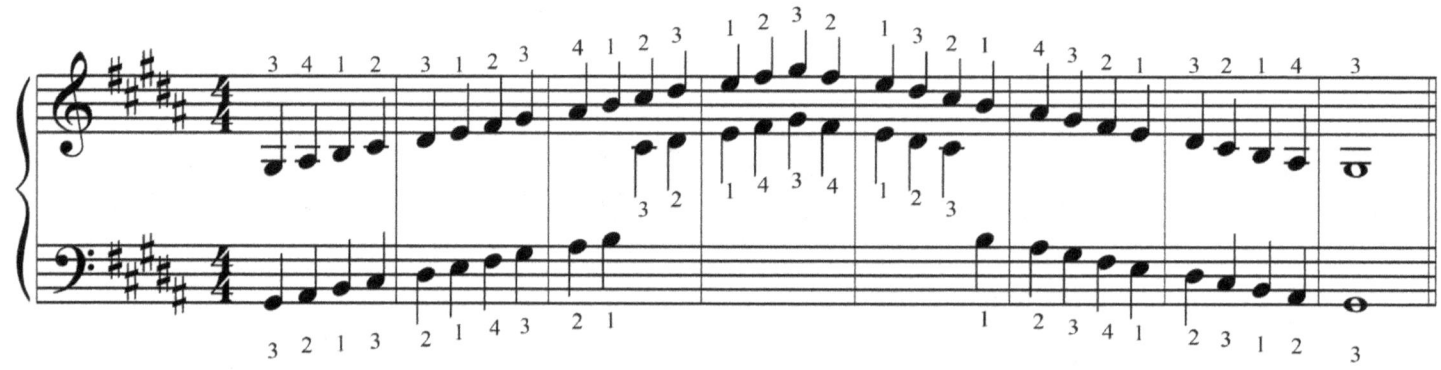

Chapter Nine – Major and Minor Arpeggios

If you know your major and minor scales, then it is easy to understand major and minor arpeggios. Arpeggios use the 1st, 3rd and 5th notes of their corresponding scale and are played in succession up and down the keyboard.

The arpeggios written in this chapter span two octaves and are placed in groups based on common fingering characteristics.

Group One

Our first group of arpeggios all use the following fingering.

R.H. 1 2 3 1 2 3 5

L.H. 5 4 2 1 4 2 1

This includes arpeggios that consist of all white notes which include:

- C Major
- G Major
- F Major

Example 9a – C Major

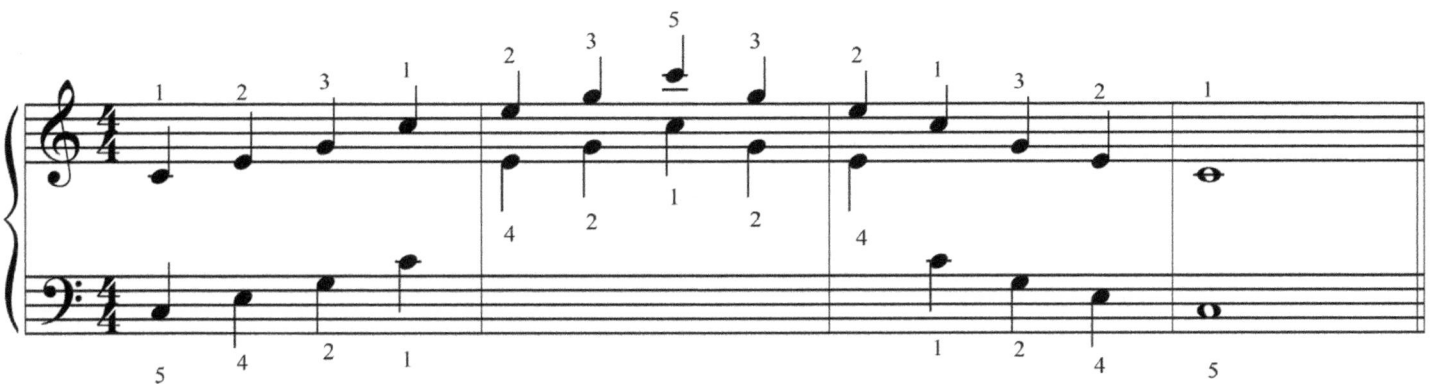

Example 9b – F Major

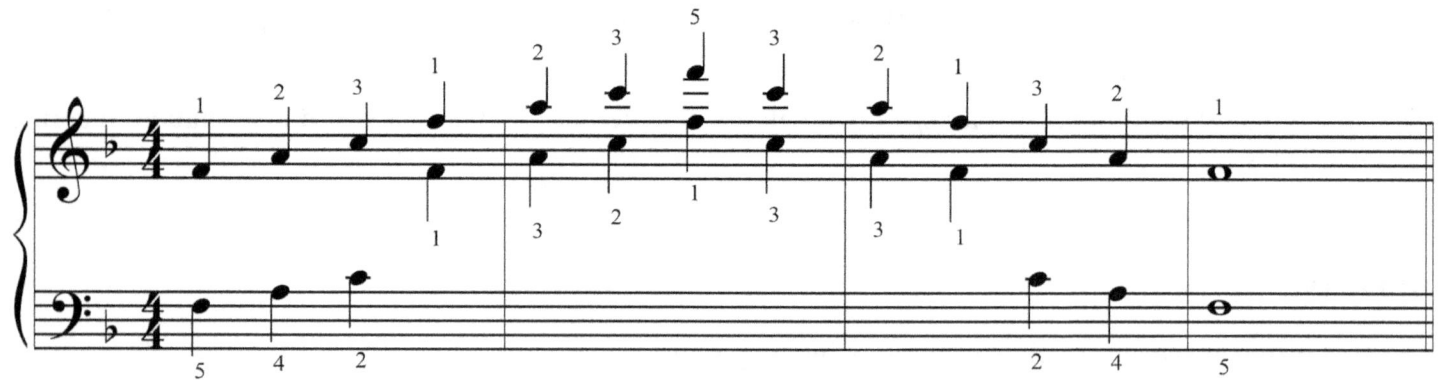

Example 9c – G Major

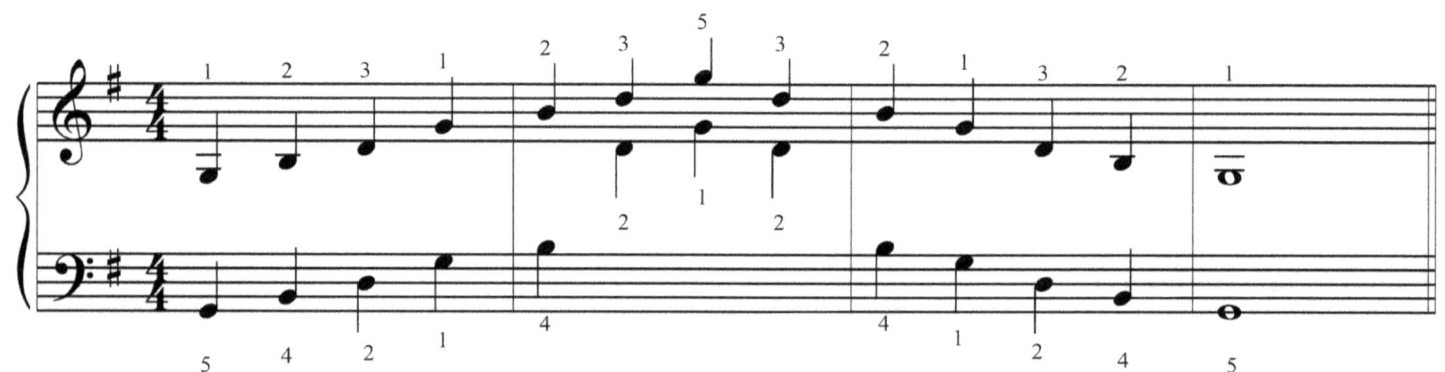

And also:

- A minor
- D minor
- E minor

Example 9d – A minor

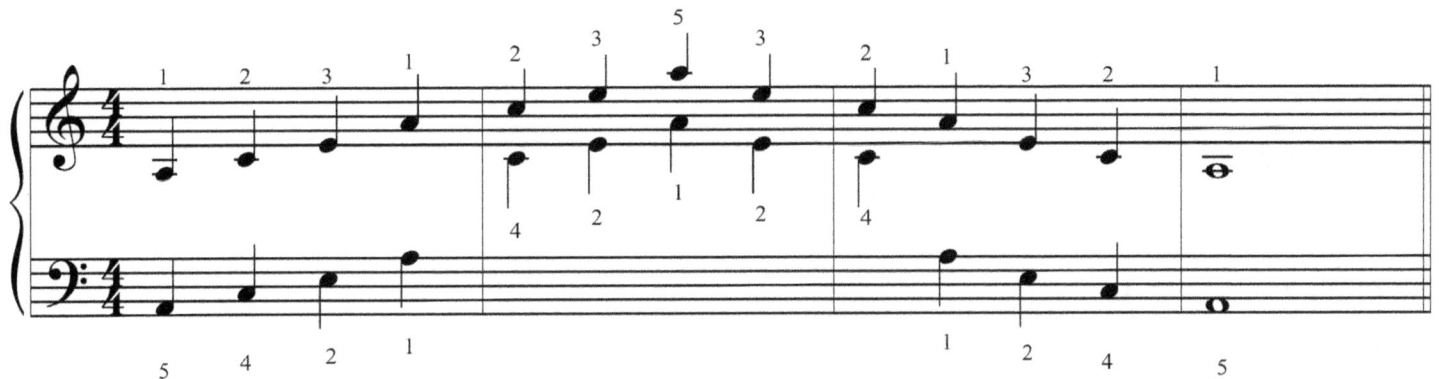

Example 9e – D minor

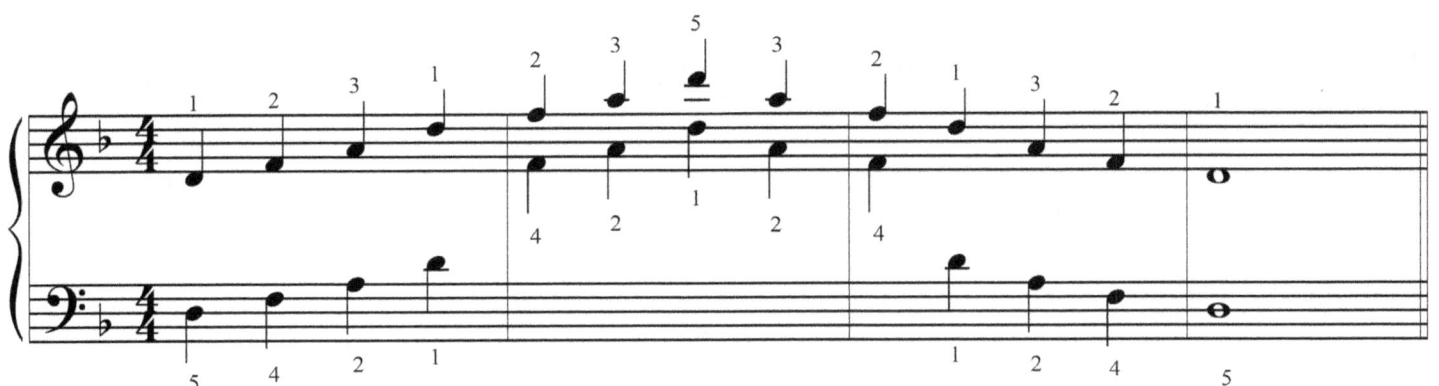

Example 9f – E minor

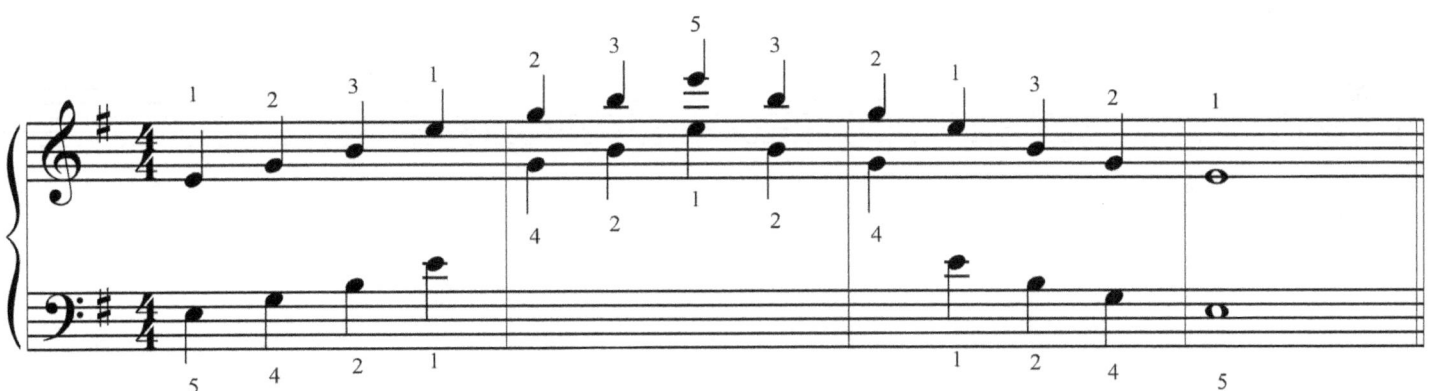

Though the arpeggios that follow do not consist of all white notes, they still use the same fingering pattern.

- C minor
- F minor
- G minor
- B minor
- E♭ minor (or D♯ minor)

Example 9g – C minor

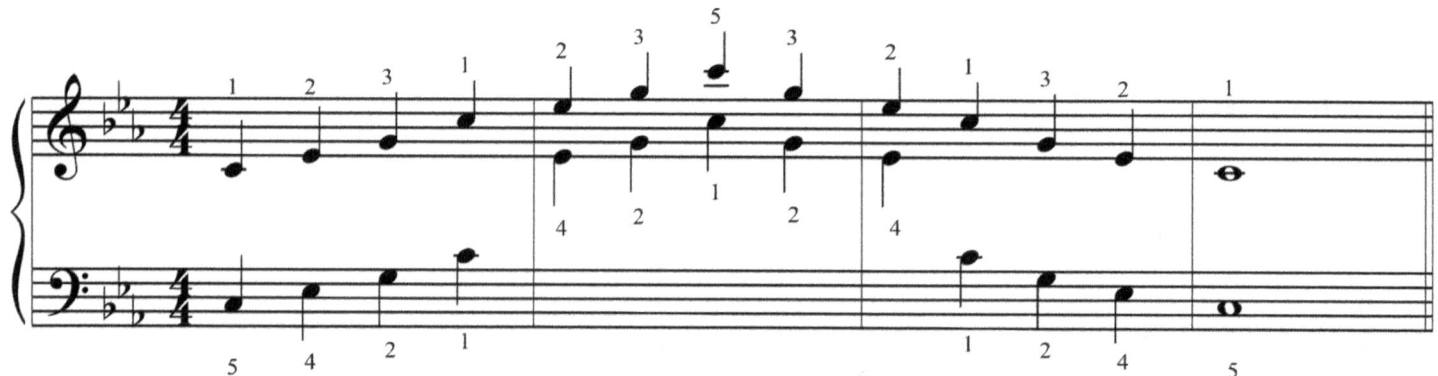

Example 9h – F minor

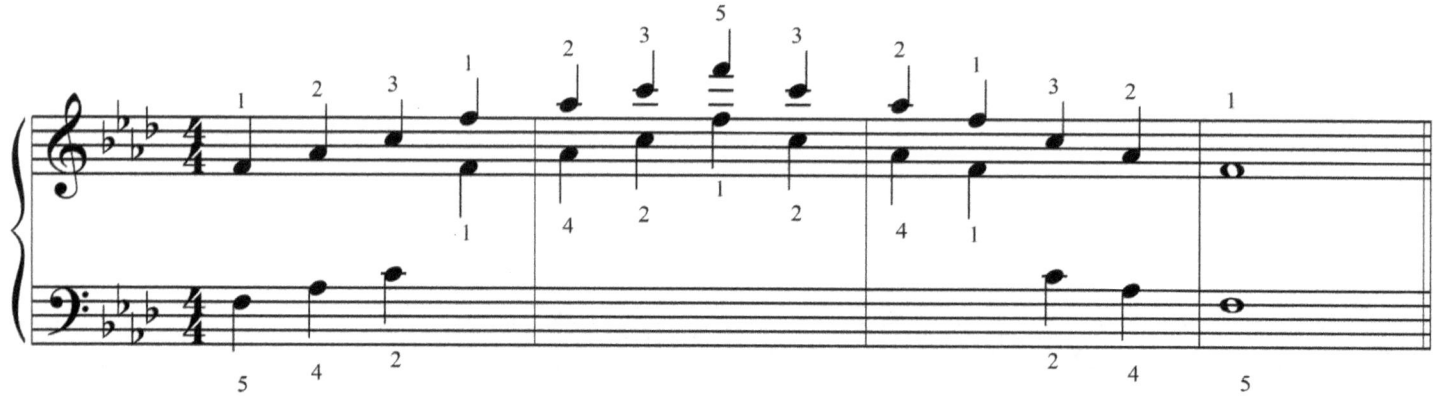

Example 9i – G minor

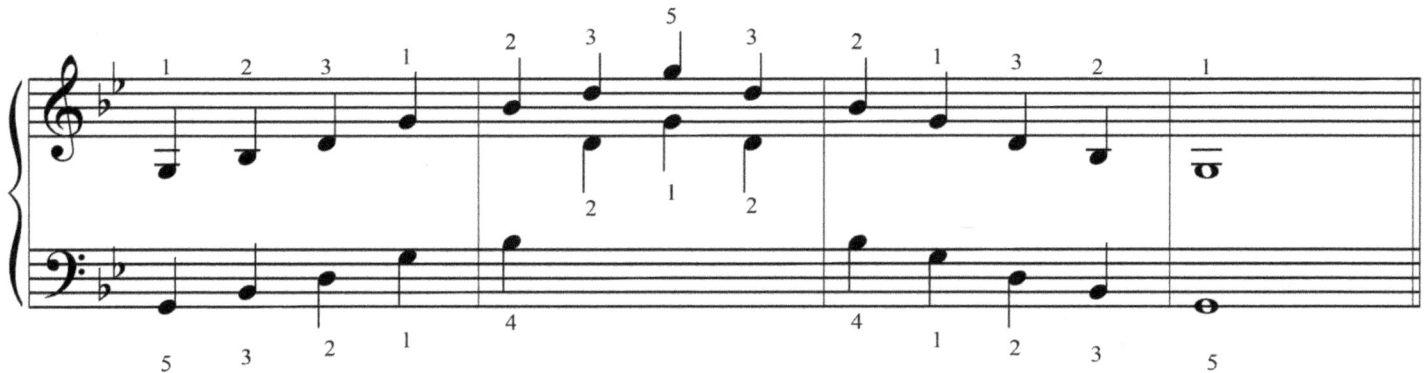

Example 9j – B minor

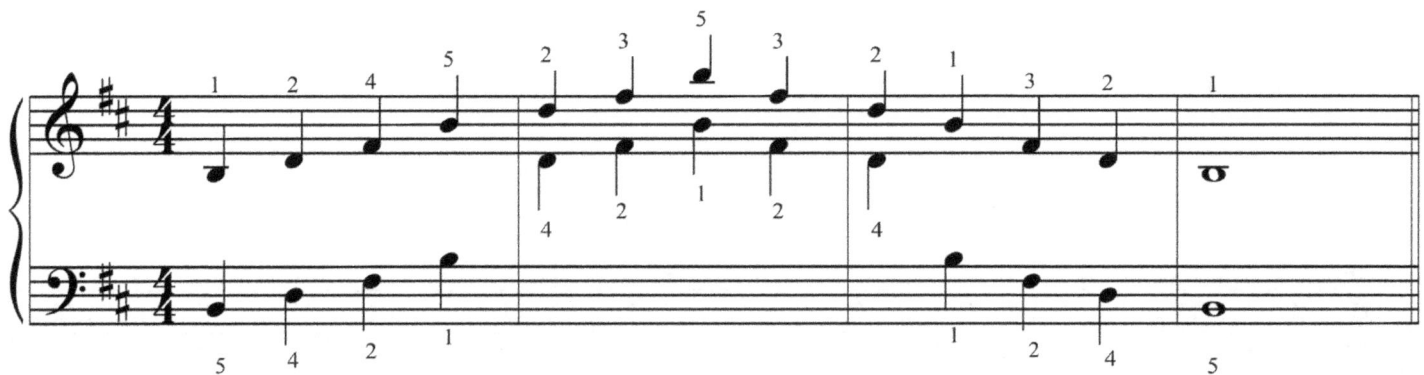

Example 9k – E♭ minor

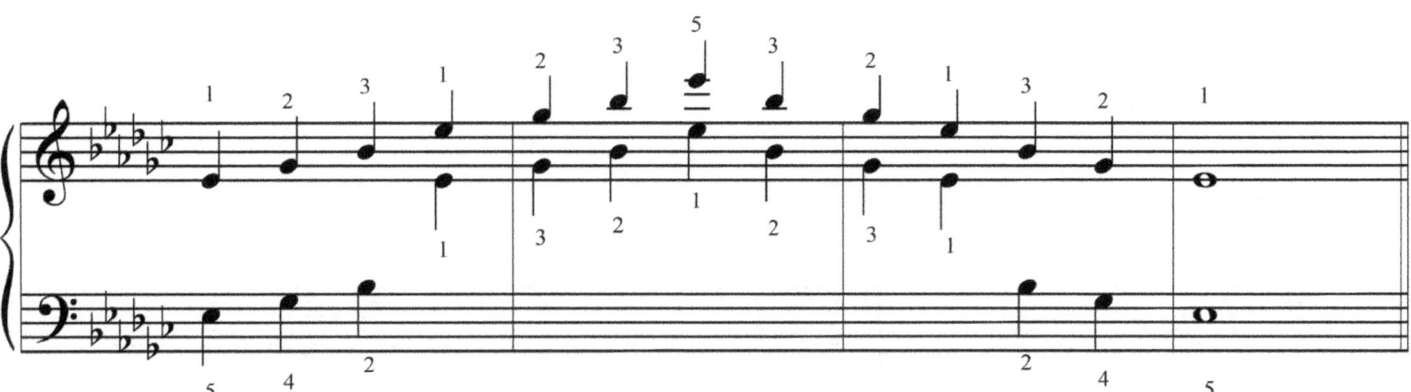

Group Two

Our second group of arpeggios has a change in the left hand fingering. The arpeggios that belong to this group include:

- D Major
- A Major
- E Major
- B Major
- G♭ Major (or F♯ Major)

These all use the following fingering.

R.H. 1 2 3 1 2 3 5

L.H. 5 3 2 1 4 2 1

Example 9l – D Major

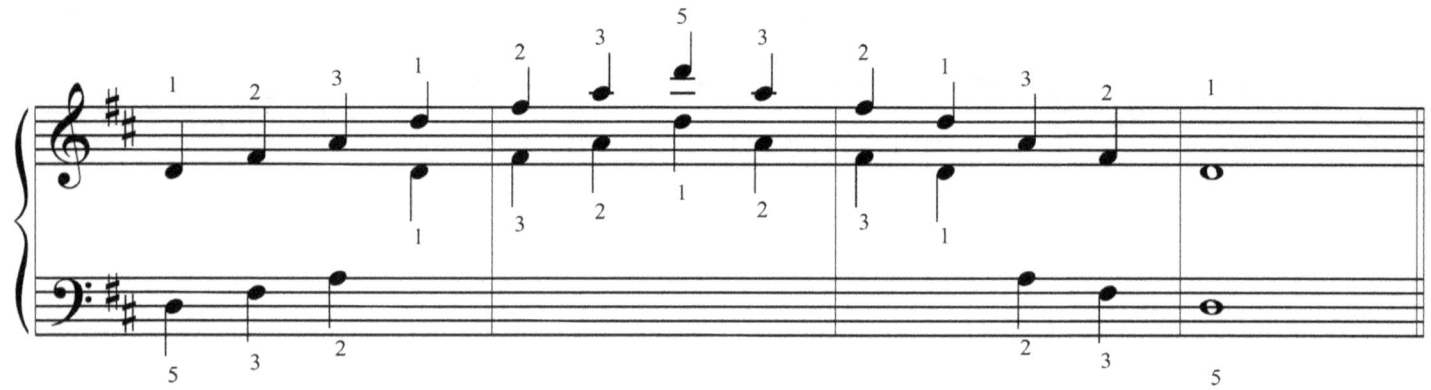

Example 9m – A Major

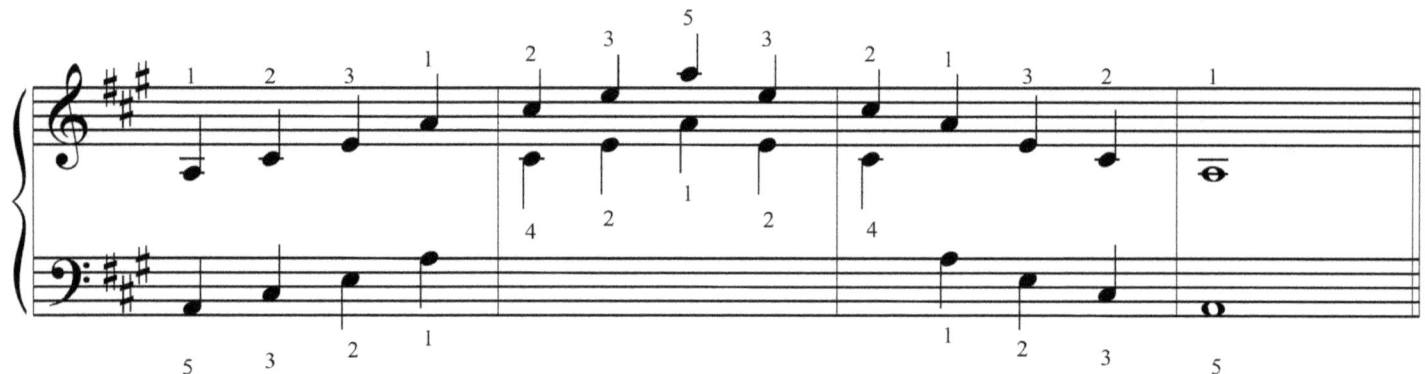

Example 9n – E Major

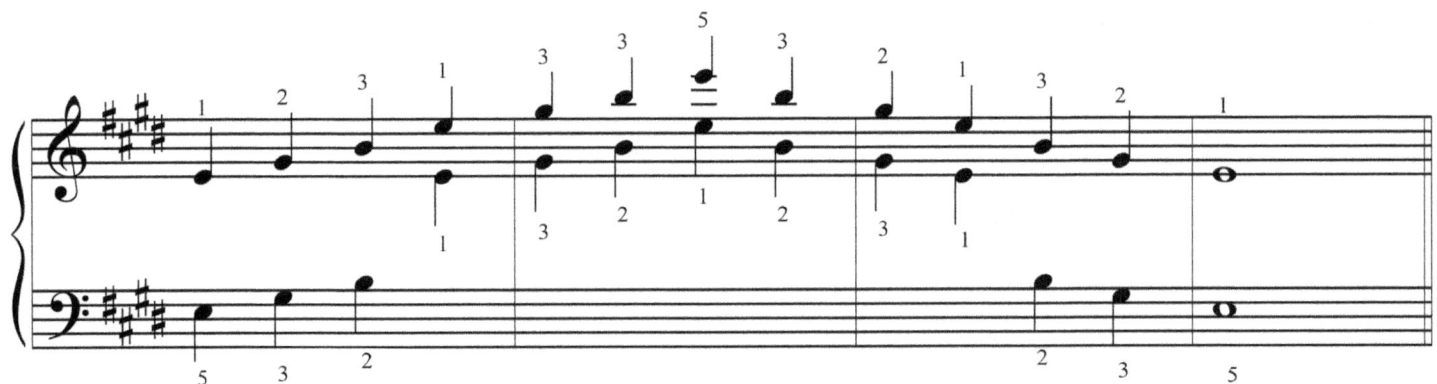

Example 9o – B Major

Example 9p – G♭ Major

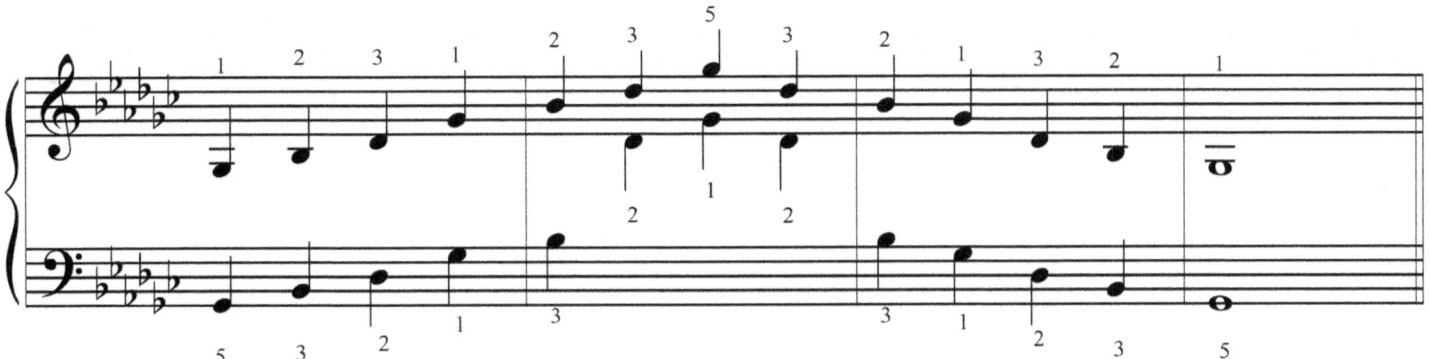

Group Three

Group three consists of arpeggios that begin on a black key, followed by the thumb which plays on the white key that immediately follows.

R.H. 4 1 2 4 1 2 4

L.H. 2 1 4 2 1 4 2

Arpeggios that belong to this group include:

- B♭ Major
- E♭ Major
- A♭ Major
- D♭ Major (C♯ Major)
- F♯ minor
- C♯ minor
- G♯ minor

Example 9q – B♭ Major

Example 9r – E♭ Major

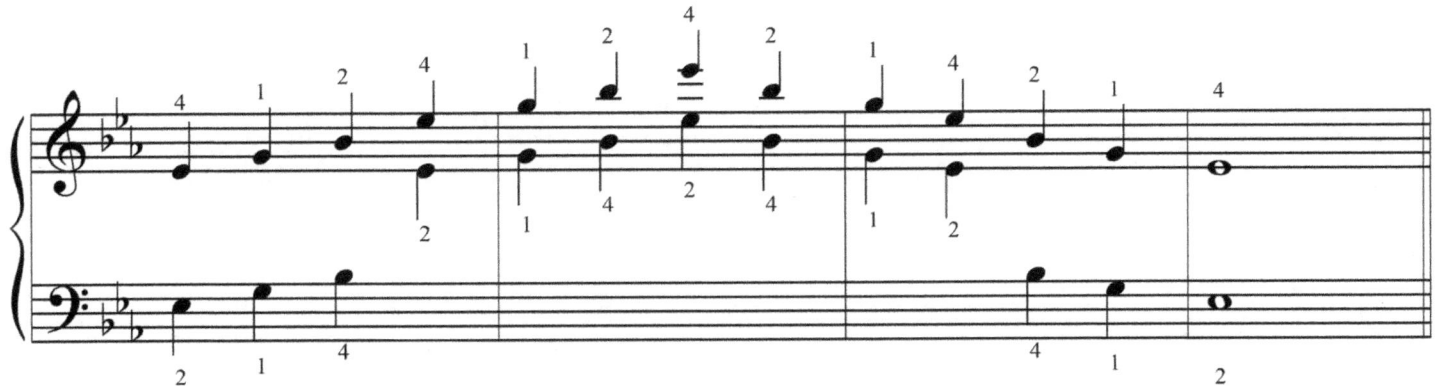

Example 9s – A♭ Major

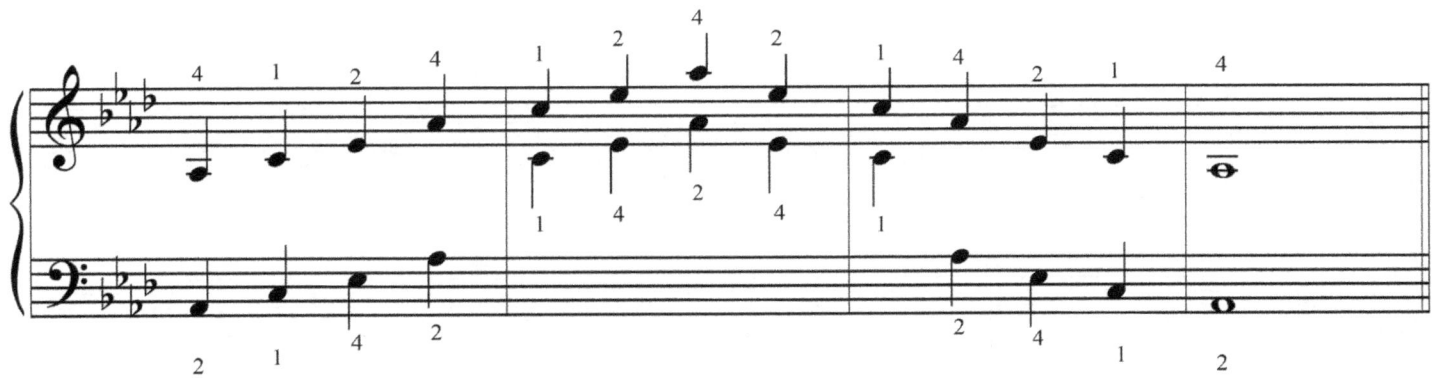

Example 9t – D♭ Major

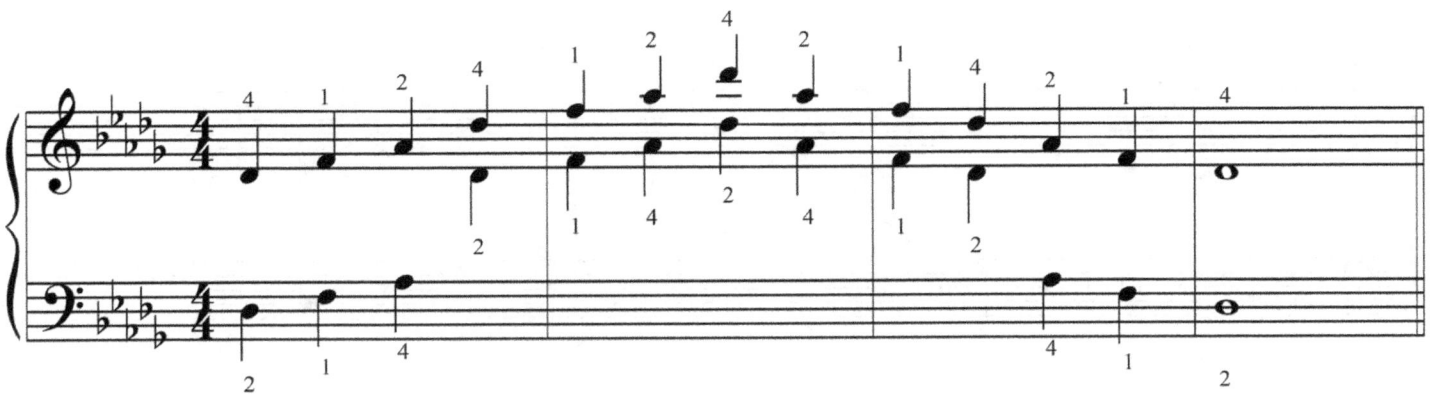

Example 9u – F# minor

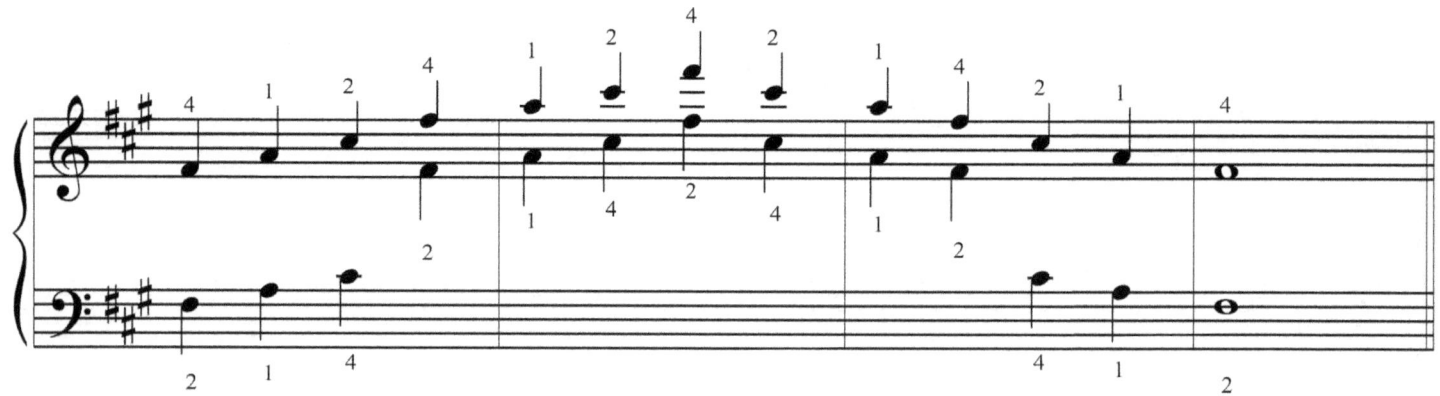

Example 9v – C# minor

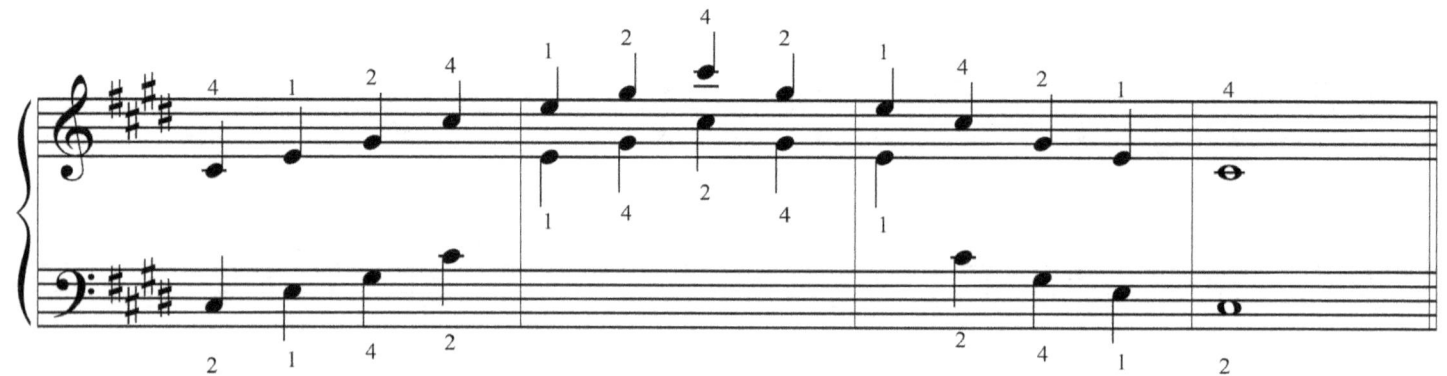

Example 9w – G# minor

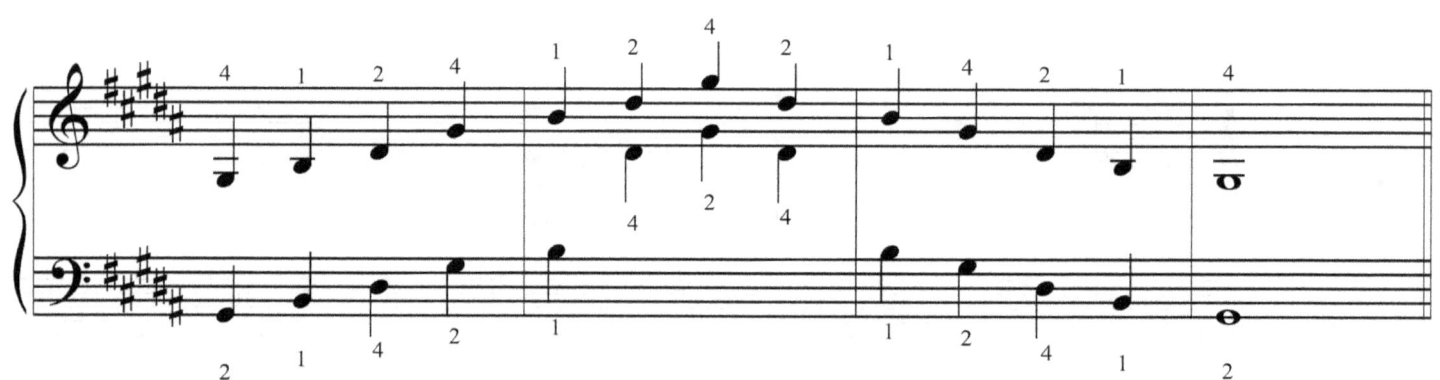

Group Four

This group contains only B♭ minor, which uses the following fingering pattern.

R.H. 2 3 1 2 3 1 2

L.H. 3 2 1 3 2 1 2

Example 9x

Conclusion and Further Practice Tips

The exercises and practice suggestions in this book can be practiced as presented or can be applied to actual piano pieces on which you are working. While it is always good to practice scales, arpeggios and other finger exercises on their own, it is even more useful to apply the same practice techniques to the passages found in the music you are studying.

For example, suppose you are working on a piece that contains a busy passage of 1/16th or 1/8th notes at a fast tempo. You can turn the notes of that passage into an actual technical exercise by practicing it staccato and with displaced rhythm as in chapters three and five.

Or perhaps you are studying a piece in which you play octaves in your right or left hand. You can certainly take that passage and apply the practice suggestions found in Chapter Six.

Whenever you sit down to practice you should always keep a few things in mind.

There is a difference between playing a piece of music and practicing it. We all enjoy playing through a piece of music, but whenever we play through a piece that we are currently learning, we often push our way through the parts that are giving us some trouble without actually treating the problem itself.

When it comes to your piano practice, first identify the problems you are experiencing when you initially play through a piece. In addition, think about what you want to be able to accomplish in this particular practice session. If a particular section or even a measure, is getting the best of you, go over it until you get it right. Check the fingering. Do you know what fingering to use or are you just using whichever finger plays at that moment? Not knowing or not following a good fingering often hinders good piano playing.

How about your hand position? Do you have a good hand shape or are your hands flat? Do you have tension in the hand or fingers? If you playing a scale-like figure away from the center of the piano, are you leading with your elbow? Go over the section in question until you have it right. Once you have accomplished that, practice leading into the section as well, so there is a smooth transition between that section and the preceding one.

It also helps to work backwards. We love to start at the beginning. Why not start toward the end of the piece instead? Divide your song or composition into sections. Suppose you have divided up your piece into four sections, and you find that the trouble spots are in the second and third section. Start with the third section first and work your way backward. Furthermore, when you practice scales and arpeggios, don't always begin ascending, begin descending as well. Oftentimes, we have an easier time ascending than descending because, just like when we play songs and compositions, we have a tendency to go back to the beginning.

Once you have worked out the trouble spots, this is when you play through the piece from beginning to end to check your progress. However, when you play through a piece, this is no longer the time to focus and work on technique. You should simply enjoy playing the music and trust that the work you put into perfecting your technique shines through in your performance

One final thought: When it comes to how long one should practice, *mind* spent always trumps *time* spent. Aim for a good quality practice session. You know when you've had a good practice session if you can see progress.

www.ingramcontent.com/pod-product-compliance
Lightning Source LLC
LaVergne TN
LVHW061254060426
835507LV00020B/2321